Technology in Supply Chain Management and Logistics

Technology in Supply Chain Management and Logistics

Current Practice and Future Applications

ANTHONY M. PAGANO
Center for Supply Chain Management and Logistics,
University of Illinois at Chicago, Chicago, IL,
United States

MATTHEW LIOTINE
Department of Information & Decision Sciences,
University of Illinois at Chicago, Chicago, IL,
United States

ELSEVIER

Elsevier
Radarweg 29, PO Box 211, 1000 AE Amsterdam, Netherlands
The Boulevard, Langford Lane, Kidlington, Oxford OX5 1GB, United Kingdom
50 Hampshire Street, 5th Floor, Cambridge, MA 02139, United States

British Library Cataloguing-in-Publication Data
A catalogue record for this book is available from the British Library

Library of Congress Cataloging-in-Publication Data
A catalog record for this book is available from the Library of Congress

ISBN: 978-0-12-815956-9

For Information on all Elsevier publications
visit our website at https://www.elsevier.com/books-and-journals

Publisher: Joe Hayton
Acquisition Editor: Brian Romer
Editorial Project Manager: Andrae Akeh
Production Project Manager: Nirmala Arumugam
Cover Designer: Mark Rogers

Typeset by MPS Limited, Chennai, India

Transferred to Digital Printing in 2019

Contents

List of contributors

Don Ginocchio
SAP University Alliances, University of Notre Dame, Notre Dame, IN, United States

Mellissa Gyimah-Concepcion
Division of Education, Judson University, Elgin, Illinois, United States

Matthew Liotine
Department of Information & Decision Sciences, University of Illinois at Chicago, Chicago, IL, United States

Sang Moon
Department of Business Administration, Hankyong National University, Anseong, South Korea

Unsal Ozdogru
Department of Information and Decision Sciences, The University of Illinois at Chicago, Chicago, IL, United States

Anthony M. Pagano
Center for Supply Chain Management and Logistics, University of Illinois at Chicago, Chicago, IL, United States

William E. Stillman
Executive Vice President and Co-owner of GAINSystems (retired)

JoAnn Verdin
Parkinson School of the Health Sciences and Public Health, Department of Healthcare Administration, Loyola University Chicago, Chicago, IL, United States

Acknowledgments

We would like to thank the authors of the individual chapters of this book for the excellent analysis and detailed discussion of technology in various aspects of supply chain management. In particular, we would like to acknowledge the contributions of Prof. Unsal Ozdogru, author of Chapter 3, Impact of exponential technologies on global supply chain management; Mr. William E. Stillman, author of Chapter 5, Technologies for dealing with error in supply chain planning, and coauthor of Chapter 9, Case studies of supply chain technology implementation; Dr. JoAnn Verdin, author of Chapter 6, Emerging technologies in the health-care supply chain; Prof. Sang Moon, author of Chapter 7, The emergence of new containers in cold chain; and Dr. Mellissa Gyimah-Concepcion, author of Chapter 10, Technology in supply-chain management and logistics: what does the future hold? We could not have been able to provide the depth of understanding of technology in supply chain without their excellent chapters.

We would especially like to acknowledge the contribution of Dr. Sungjin Kim, former President of Hankyong National University, South Korea, whose vision to fund a study of technology in supply chain management in the United States led to much of the research that is the basis for this book.

Thank you all and hope you get a lot out of this book.

Anthony M. Pagano
Matthew Liotine

CHAPTER 1

Introduction

While there are a number of college textbooks related to specific areas within logistics and supply chain issues, there are very few general supply chain management books dealing exclusively with technology in supply chain management. We could find only one book dealing with technology, and it was published in 2010. Much has changed since then. There is an untapped college market for a supply chain and logistics book that uses examples of the use of technology. Indeed, undergraduate and graduate business schools are increasing their course offerings in logistics and supply chain management due to student demand. Supply chain managers' salaries are increasing, and c-level positions are being added to many companies. To meet this demand, these new courses will require updated and relevant books that provide timely perspectives and examples using "real-world" situations.

Additionally, professionals working in the field need to stay current on the trends and issues facing supply chain management. They will be leading their organizations' strategies on supply chain management. This book would feed their position as thought leaders looking to make their supply chain leaner, more visionary, and reflective of the trends in supply chain management. The book can also be used in executive education courses in supply chain and logistics management.

The objectives of this book include:

- Identifying the emerging technologies, either hardware or software, that companies are investing in, currently and in the short term.
- Understanding the implications of the technologies with respect to areas that include value creation, operational effectiveness, investment level, technical migration, and general industry acceptance.
- Identifying short-term trends in technology acceptance and utilization levels across various industry sectors.
- Characterizing the supply chain and logistics applications in which the technologies are being utilized for product planning, materials management, and inventory, transportation, distribution, workflow, plant maintenance, quality assurance, environment, and health and safety.

Technology in Supply Chain Management and Logistics
DOI: https://doi.org/10.1016/B978-0-12-815956-9.00001-6

- Developing a reference base that supply chain professionals can utilize to guide future technology investment decisions, including procurement of best value technologies and how they can best be used for logistics operations.

Additionally, this book includes recent technological developments and applications of technology in a variety of areas including blockchain, Internet of Things (IoT), inventory optimization, and medical supply chain. Case studies of the use of technology in supply chain management are included.

The book utilizes a set of YouTube videos on the application of each of the technologies. The videos are embedded in the text. These videos help to illustrate how each of the technologies are utilized. The videos supplement the written material to provide the reader with virtual experience in the use of the technology.

Until recently, technology has been considered as an enabler for improvements in underlying supply chain and logistics operations. However, recent trends in society and business such as mobile computing, social media, and online retailing have significantly changed almost every aspect of the supply chain and logistics landscape. In Chapter 2, Technologies in Supply Chain Management and Logistics, by Anthony M. Pagano and Matthew Liotine, the following technologies were found to have a pervasive role in altering this landscape:

- Maturing Technologies
  - Optimization software
  - Sensors/telematics
  - Cloud computing
  - Data warehouse and integration
  - Automated storage and retrieval
- Growth Technologies
  - Mobility
  - Wearability
  - Data analytics
  - Social media
- Emerging Technologies
  - 3D Printing
  - Drones
  - Autonomous vehicles
- Exponential Technologies
  - Blockchain
  - IoT

- Virtual reality
- Machine learning

Each of these technologies is discussed, along with videos illustrating their use.

Chapter 3 is titled "Impact of Exponential Technologies on Global Supply Chain Management," by Unsal Ozdogru. Technology has been rapidly evolving over the last several decades, revolutionizing all industries such as communication, transportation, education, health care, life sciences, energy, and retail, among many others. This momentum has created many opportunities for companies in their supply chain to expand their business globally to gain competitive advantage, ultimately increasing their profitability. Several leading technologies including blockchain, IoT, virtual/augmented/extended reality (VR/AR/XR), machine learning, 3D Printing among others, have been identified as having a significant influence on global supply chain operations. In this chapter, Professor Ozdogru surveys the literature on the implications of technologies in terms of their potential value creation including increasing profit, improving efficiency and agility, reducing cost and lead times, and increasing visibility and eliminating waste in global supply chain management. Based on the findings, she identifies the challenges and limitations of these technologies within global supply chain operations.

Blockchain is the topic of Chapter 4, The Supply Blockchain: Integrating Blockchain Technology within Supply Chain Operations, which is written by Matthew Liotine. Blockchain is a distributed system of record that employs a trust protocol built on elements of networking and cryptology. Blockchain can improve the speed of transaction execution and validation across multiple parties. These include digitally validating a transaction that has occurred between two entities and rendering it irrefutable. When one considers the numerous kinds and volume of supply chain transactions that occur daily, this fundamental capability can have profound impacts. Having readily available information that is trustworthy can streamline activities such as purchasing, contracting and qualifying materials. This chapter surveys some current applications of blockchain by early industry adopters and explores additional potential applications for supply chain operations. It concludes with a prescriptive approach for how enterprises can determine and identify effective implementation scenarios for blockchain in their supply chain operations.

The science of inventory optimization is the topic of Chapter 5, Technologies for Dealing with Error in Supply Chain Planning, written by William Stillman. To consistently achieve the "Perfect Order," with the maximum contribution to margin, one needs to plan across the enterprise at the most granular level. This means planning at the item or SKU level for every location (SKUL) where inventory is held or used. The Science of IO envelops every aspect of the enterprise where any piece of inventory rests or passes through. When management plans to deliver the "Perfect Order," they need to incorporate, comprehensively, every element of the enterprise simultaneously; every component of the enterprise—down to the smallest SKUL—is subject to change at any time. Therefore, to consistently achieve the "Perfect Order," management needs to comprehensively Monitor, Analyze, and Plan (MAP) all policies, plans, and actions for the enterprise, at every SKUL level, every day.

Chapter 6, Emerging Technologies in the Health Care Supply Chain, written by JoAnn Verdin, concerns emerging technologies in the health care supply chain. In this chapter, the background and organization of the health care supply chain are reviewed, and the impact of emerging technologies are described. Maturing technologies including optimization software, sensors/telematics, cloud computing, data warehouse systems, and automated storage and retrieval are examined. Growth technologies including mobility, wearable devices, data analytics, and social media are examined as they potentially relate to the health care supply chain. Emerging technologies including 3D printing, drone delivery, and autonomous vehicles are presented and examples provided on their use in the health care supply chain. Exponential technologies including blockchain, the IoT, Virtual/Augmented Reality, and Artificial Intelligence (AI) are described with regard to potential applications that impact the health care supply chain. Future changes in the external environment of health care including decentralization, new competitors, and the increased use of telemedicine are described with respect to impacts on the health care supply chain.

Chapter 7, The Emergence of New Containers in Cold Chain, written by Sang Moon, discusses "new containers in cold chain" and reviews recently introduced containers such as CA (Controlled Atmosphere) containers and high-insulated containers. Because of the high demand for fresh foods and changes in cold chain environments, efforts to extend the shelf life of these foods have resulted in the development of new technology that reduces transportation costs. This chapter focuses on how these containers are impacting the overall cold chain, by reviewing several case studies. CA containers are used to supplement reefer containers. High-insulated containers are developed to enhance insulating performance.

The impact of these containers on cold chain and food trade are discussed in this chapter.

Chapter 8, Unlocking Digital Innovation: Guiding Principles for Driving Digital Technology in the Supply Chain, written by Matthew Liotine, is entitled "Unlocking Digital Innovation: Guiding Principles for Driving Digital Technology in the Supply Chain." Innovating supply chain operations with digital technology is a challenge for many enterprises due to ingrained barriers. Yet, innovation is a necessity that goes beyond continuous improvement. This chapter defines what innovation means and reviews the barriers typically encountered in innovating supply chain operations. It reviews the trends in innovation methods and how they can be used to drive changes in supply chain operations. Two general types of innovation are reviewed: funnel methods and rocket methods. Funnel methods are widely used for new product development and often exhibit low success rates. Such approaches are being supplanted by newer, "rocket," methods which are goal oriented. These methods are faster and can be adapted for both product and process innovation. An example of a rocket method is profiled using a "canvas approach." Appraisal of the outcome of these methods is reviewed using common business case metrics.

Case studies of supply chain technology implementation are presented in Chapter 9, Case Studies of Supply Chain Technology Implementation. Written by Anthony M. Pagano, Matthew Liotine and William Stillman, this chapter is comprised of a series of case studies of specific companies that used and integrated one or more of the technologies, identified in the previous chapters, into their supply chain and logistics operations. This was accomplished by interviewing a select sample of firms to identify the type of technology they have implemented, the problems involved in implementation, user training necessary, and how this new technology interfaced with technology currently in use in the business, among other issues. The first part of the chapter discusses five different companies that implemented several of the technologies discussed in earlier chapters in this book. The companies asked not to be identified. The last part of the chapter discusses three companies which implemented inventory optimization software. The results, including impacts on cost savings, operations, and inventory management are examined.

The last decade of the 20th century has been quite transient and dynamic for organizations and businesses, particularly so in the supply chain management field. The rate of change is increasing as we progress into the 21st century, and with that, organizations have had to be responsive to this change—and at a rapid pace! Chapter 10, Technology in Supply Chain Management and Logistics: What Does the Future Hold?, written by Mellissa Gyimah-Concepcion, focuses on the future of technology in the supply chain, and this involves companies, as well as classrooms and courses. It is a cutting-edge notion that is only just getting recognized within the supply chain, and being explored and utilized in a way that is invigorating and unique, not recreating old systems with new technology endeavors. We utilize a focus group of Board member companies of the Center for Supply Chain Management and Logistics at the University of Illinois at Chicago to understand what does the future hold.

CHAPTER 2

Technologies in supply chain management and logistics

Anthony M. Pagano[1] and Matthew Liotine[2]
[1]Center for Supply Chain Management and Logistics, University of Illinois at Chicago, Chicago, IL, United States
[2]Department of Information & Decision Sciences, University of Illinois at Chicago, Chicago, IL, United States

Contents

Technology in Supply Chain Management and Logistics
DOI: https://doi.org/10.1016/B978-0-12-815956-9.00002-8

Introduction

This research, undertaken by the University of Illinois at Chicago's Center for Supply Chain Management and Logistics, involves a multiyear study that works toward analyzing the recent technological trends in the logistics and supply chain management space in the United States, which are being followed by major corporations. The objectives of this chapter are to

- identify the emerging technologies, either hardware or software, in which companies are investing, currently and in the short term;
- understand the implications of the technologies with respect to areas that include value creation, operational effectiveness, investment level, technical migration, and general industry acceptance;
- identify short-term trends in the technology acceptance and utilization levels across various industry sectors;
- characterize the supply chain and logistics applications in which the technologies are being utilized in product planning, materials management and inventory, transportation, distribution, workflow, plant maintenance, quality assurance, environment, health, and safety; and
- identify favored suppliers for the technologies identified.

Supply chain business trends

Supply chains are now used to support a company's business strategies. Most companies recognize their supply chain is a key business process versus a cost center, as what was thought of in the past. Distribution networks are evolving from centralized to distributed and then to hybrid. Companies are also utilizing multimode logistics and transportation instead of a single mode. In addition, more companies are shipping directly to their customers, in addition to channel shipping. These trends have resulted in the growth in supply chain risk, including disruptions due to adverse events.

These trends lead to a variety of challenges including the need for improving communication with suppliers, multisourcing of goods and services, careful safety stock auditing, improved risk planning techniques, and the diversification of offering and the customer base. Further, more firms are placing an emphasis on social and environmental responsibility, which can lead to a positive brand image, stricter regulatory compliance, improved energy resource utilization, and reduced material consumption. Technology can help companies meet these challenges.

Motivation for supply chain technology investments

Overall, companies have been integrating new technologies in their supply chain and logistics operations for numerous reasons. Among these are

- to improve return on investment (ROI) by using technologies that better leverage utilization of capital expenditures in people and equipment;
- to create operational efficiencies in order to reduce inventory and improve cycle times; and
- to improve customer responsiveness by reducing lead times, improving product availability, reducing stockouts, and offering flexibility to changing customer demands.

All the above mentioned reasons ultimately result in creating greater value for the customer base, and consequently improved profitability. To this end, companies are seeking ways to establish greater end-to-end visibility across the complexity of supply chain and logistics operations, processes, and systems. Visibility provides "controlled access and transparency to accurate, timely and complete events and data (transactions, content and relevant supply chain information) within and across organizations and to support effective planning and execution of supply chain operations" (Titze & Barger, 2015).

Fig. 2.1 illustrates these relationships as they existed at the outset of this study.

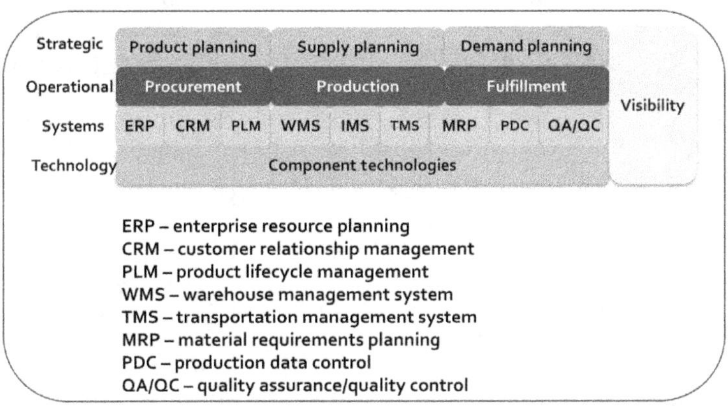

Figure 2.1 Supply Chain and Logistics Relationships.

Vendor interviews

We interviewed a group of 10 companies that provide various innovative technological services for industry giants in North America and elsewhere. The choice of vendors was based on the innovative quality of their product/service, its usability and adaptability in relation to current supply chain practices, and associated ROI. Whenever possible, the companies were visited personally. For companies situated elsewhere, video conferencing or conference calls were chosen as the mode of interviewing.

The contents of these meetings were documented and serve as the basis for part of the discussions in this chapter. A list of companies interviewed is shown in Table 2.1, along with their associated field of service in the supply chain space. While there is much diversity in the services and products provided by these companies, they all contribute to optimizing complex, global supply chains. A comprehensive view of how these

Table 2.1 List of technology vendors interviewed

Company Name	Services	Website
SAP	Enterprise Resource Planning	http://www.sap.com/index.html
Vuzix	Hardware—for Optimized Warehouse Operations	http://www.vuzix.com/
ORTEC	Software Solutions—Advanced Planning and Optimization	http://ortec.com/
Aberdeen Group	Industry Research	http://www.aberdeen.com/
Accenture	Management Consulting and Technology Services	http://www.accenture.com/
Mecalux	Industrial, Racking & Storage Solutions	http://www.interlakemecalux.com/
GT Nexus	Cloud-Based Supply Chain Services	http://www.gtnexus.com/
Bastian Solutions	Material-Handling Systems Integrator	http://www.bastiansolutions.com/
AGV Solutions	Automated Guided Vehicle Systems Provider	http://agvsolutions.com/
Zebra Technologies	Tracking Technology and Solutions	https://www.zebra.com

different technologies interact with each other to have a positive impact on the supply chain operations is provided in this chapter.

Supply chain technology areas

Until recently, technology has been considered an enabler for improvements in underlying supply chain and logistics operations. However, recent trends in society and business, such as mobile computing, social media, and online retailing, have significantly changed almost every aspect of the supply chain and logistics landscape. In this study the following technologies were found to have a pervasive role in altering this landscape:

- Maturing technologies

  Based on industry study, the following technologies are considered maturing technologies, whose aim is to improve service and efficiency.

  - Optimization software
  - Sensors/Telematics
  - Cloud computing
  - Data warehouse and integration
  - Automated storage (AS) and retrieval

  Current adoption levels for these technologies are at 35% and are projected to reach 80%–90% by 2019 (MHI, 2015).

- Growth technologies

  The following technologies are considered growth technologies, whose adoption rates are currently about 20%, but are expected to grow steadily in the next 3–5 years (MHI, 2015).

  - Mobility
  - Wearability
  - Data analytics
  - Social media

- Emerging technologies

  The following technologies are considered emerging technologies, with current adoption rates of 10% (MHI, 2015). These technologies are viewed as disruptive in nature and thus have the potential significantly to alter supply chain and logistics operations in unforeseen ways:

  - 3D printing
  - Drones
  - Autonomous vehicles

- Exponential technologies

  These are technologies that have just begun to make their way into general use in supply chain management.
  - Blockchain
  - Internet of Things
  - Virtual reality (VR)
  - Machine learning

Study findings

It is important to note that the impacts of the abovementioned technologies in many cases are collective rather than individual, a result of integrating a technology with one or more of the others. The following sections briefly describe their impacts as identified in this chapter.

Cloud computing

Cloud computing technology has enabled companies to migrate platforms and applications that were once predominantly on-premises or within public/private cloud environments. Cloud computing is a technology that provides user applications that are delivered from a collected group of distributed computing resources (e.g., servers, databases, applications, and networks). Cloud computing offerings have been classified into Software as a Service (SaaS), Platform as a Service (PaaS), and Infrastructure as a Service (IaaS). SaaS consumers use a provider's applications running on a cloud infrastructure, accessing them using various client devices through a thin client interface such as a web browser. The underlying cloud infrastructure includes networks, servers, operating systems, and storage, which are invisible to the customer. SaaS providers are likely to be PaaS consumers, paying for memory, storage environments, and tools when they create SaaS applications. PaaS providers are consumers of IaaS providers, who offer cloud resources as virtualized resources pools, again masking the underlying computing and communications infrastructure, which comprise the cloud.

The benefits of cloud computing include lower implementation costs, faster time to value, and cost-effective upgrades, among others. The capital savings that cloud computing offers has made rapid deployment of ubiquitous information sharing solutions more cost effective. The use of private clouds has enabled the orchestration of capacity sharing and management across the various players in a supply chain. Clouds can be multienterprise in nature and thus provide a group of supply chain partners at different tiers with controlled, real-time access and transparency to data events. Clouds provide the ability for multiple enterprises to access and share information, such as inventory, capacity, and logistics data. Transportation management systems (TMS) have been cloud oriented for some time, but warehouse management systems (WMS) have been slow to move to the cloud, due to insufficient response times when connecting to terminal and material-handling systems. However, it is envisioned that this trend will change with technology improvements.

As an example, GT Nexus provides a solution for making use of the vast amounts of data that are collected in a supply chain, often using big data approaches. It offers a cloud-based platform for companies in a supply chain to share logistics data in real time. The cloud platform serves as data hub in which companies are brought to the data and not the other way around. This provides the full visibility of updated data across the supply chain.

For instance, status information regarding orders and shipments is maintained on the cloud so that it can be used to monitor the flow across suppliers and/or logistic service providers and to circulate alert notifications if any disruption occurs. Over time, notifications can collectively be used to help brand certain suppliers or service providers, thus enabling firms to manage risks better.

Another example of the use of clouds in supply chains is in collaborative sourcing, which is multiple bidding over one central cloud platform (Noosh, Inc, 2014). Implemented as a SaaS approach, this approach is envisioned to gradually replace older, traditional sourcing methods. Cloud-based collaborative sourcing can save organizations an average of 20.7% (McKeefry, 2014). The GT Nexus network can track supplier and buyer history and credit strength, which can be used to better assess risk.

The web link given sheds some additional light on the application of cloud computing in supply chains:

Moving supply chain to the cloud https://www.youtube.com/watch?v=ae_DKNwK_ms

Mobility

Mobility has spawned greater variability in customer demand patterns that have greatly influenced warehouse and delivery operations. In addition, mobility has also offered the ability to influence customer buying through customer location awareness using GPS. For example, by establishing presence zones in retail stores via Wi-Fi, retailers can offer promotions to a customer's mobile device based on their location.

Mobile technology provides a number of additional capabilities for supply chain and logistics at a much lower cost than traditional technologies. These include capabilities such as barcode scanning, document management, GPS tracking, real-time field work force management, shipment tracking, and real-time proof of delivery. Many of these technologies can now be implemented using widely available smartphones and tablets.

In addition, the data derived from mobile devices and connected businesses provides a feed for predictive analytics. For example, equipment and vehicle breakdowns can be anticipated, or a series of events that needs further investigation can be flagged. This enables organizations to convert unplanned, expensive maintenance into planned downtime, thereby improving efficiency and cost-effectiveness (Phillips, 2015).

Companies have recently started to adopt enterprise mobility solutions for improved supply chain visibility and traceability. With real-time information available to key supply chain personnel, better and more accurate decision-making is made possible. For example, identifying the problem points in a supply chain, and consequently arriving at an informed solution, becomes easier. To meet this demand, enterprise mobility platforms have sprung up, with mobile technology becoming increasingly cheaper.

The following web links provide more information on the impacts of mobility in the supply chain:

MCL Enterprise Mobility Platform https://www.youtube.com/watch?v=wSis03cW9II

Future of Mobility in Supply Chain https://www.youtube.com/watch?v=WcXWo2zT2bs

Wearability

Wearable technology moves applications and apps away from mobile phones and devices to enable hands-free voice and gesture-driven movements in warehouse and field service operations. The SAP interview revealed such trends as they are being used in warehouses. One such trend is the use of smart glasses for enhanced workflow, specifically the M100, designed by Vuzix purposefully for effective warehouse operations. Augmented reality (AR) applications designed for the smart glass environment will help in better coordination among employees to cut down on task completion time and other benefits.

Wearable technology, such as smart glasses, can enhance worker's accuracy, reduce mistakes, and improve safety for frontline workers. Adoption levels for both mobile and wearable technology are currently at 23% and are expected to reach 64% in the next 3–5 years (MHI, 2015).

There is in an increased demand for migrating from smartphone- and tablet-based AR applications to wearable devices. Companies, such as BMW, Audi, Boeing, and Airbus, are trying to achieve this for their designed applications. Vuzix makes this possible through its smart glass products, especially the M100. The M100 smart glass provides an enhanced workflow, especially in the industrial, medical, and retail sectors, by providing a hands-free experience and also enhancing capability. The M100 is an Android-based device.

The M100 has three modes of operation, they are as follows:

1. The normal mode of operation where the Android applications run on the M100 processor. Play Store applications designed for Android-based smartphones and tablets will run on the device without a problem. But further optimization is required for it to be seamlessly integrated into the smart glass environment.
2. The laptop displays operation where the device connects to laptops or personal computers and shows the display of the connected device instead.
3. Handshaking with other devices for real-time information transfer.

The battery life of the M100 had to be traded off for size since the device has to be very light for prolonged usage. But there is an option of an additional battery that increases the expected battery life. With the current specifications the device is expected to run for around 8 hours of usage without video streaming or power-draining AR applications. With video streaming and applications, this comes down to around 2 hours of heavy usage. But with the additional battery, this can be extended to 2 days.

The device has to undergo specific absorption rates, FCC testing, and other regulatory exercises. There are other obstacles that have to be tackled, such as the wearability issue, which have to be addressed in the case of people with prescription lenses. Security is another major concern as information is quite easy to access through the glasses.

Customers of Vuzix (usually enterprises) in general either write their own code (for customized applications) or work with companies that partner with Vuzix to provide for this demand. Middleware and front-end development are very expensive, especially when the need for customization must be taken into account. Vuzix is partnering with SAP for this purpose. SAP has taken up the middleware and front-end development requirement. It has recently announced two AR applications that help simplify and improve the user experience and work processes by offering a hands-free working experience: SAP AR Warehouse Picker and SAP AR Service Technician applications. These applications that boast doubled efficiency, hence allowing warehouse picking to be done twice as fast as current methods, are in demand with companies, such as DHL, FedEx, Pepsi, Coke, and Walmart.

The selling point of the M100 is that it is responsive to voice and gesture instead of the standard keyboard–based entry. This allows for a hands-free experience that is quite preferred in warehouse environments. But Android applications still need to be optimized to make better usage of these devices' capabilities. Vuzix is willing to provide the application programming interfaces for development of such applications to customers. Another advantage is that the device will save money ultimately since it replaces technology in current usage, such as barcode scanners, with powerful video and image processing functionalities. Migration is hence not a huge issue, since Vuzix is willing to provide for software customization in an advisory capacity. Vuzix also provides a very user-friendly interface. This is helpful for the workers who need to adopt an entirely new system of operation. Since the user interface is intuitive, employees do not need an extensive training period for this transition. The M100 provides 10–15 voice commands by default, but additional libraries can be used if required.

The following links provide demonstrations of smart glass wearable technology:

Future of Field Service https://www.youtube.com/watch?v = UlpGDrSmg38

Another approach is voice. KPM, which is a distributor of outdoor power equipment in the Northeast United States, relies on Lydia plug and play voice solutions from topVox. The worker wears a headset to hear directions and respond (Maloney, 2015).

Data analytics

Data analytics involves the manipulation and computation of large volumes of data, often from a wide variety of different sources.

Manipulation and computation are performed at high velocity to identify patterns, correlations, and other useful information. Data analytics capabilities have been found to enhance the utility of the mass amounts of data that can be collected and communicated through the supply chain on a regular basis. Not only can information be distilled more quickly but models can also be developed to aid decision-making at both higher and lower levels in the supply chain. Examples include:

- understanding buyer/supplier behavior to reduce inventory levels;
- using predictive analytics to predict maintenance events in equipment so that parts and labor resources can be effectively prepositioned for repairs;
- using analytics to support real-time dynamic decision-making as to how to pick and ship orders based on the current situational awareness of demand patterns; and
- creating online promotions hourly, based on buying demand to reduce inventory levels.

The current adoption level for predictive analytics is 25% and is expected to reach 70% in 3–5 years, and up to 77% in 6 years (MHI, 2015). The strategic use of data analytics has been to provide up-to-date information to make decisions and respond appropriately. Doing so can enhance agility to respond to uncertain market conditions. This feature can help reduce risk, especially in emerging markets where volatile conditions can complicate growth and production (Degun, 2014).

In the transportation sector, there has been a shift from using traditional TMS to their integration with decision-making analytics tools, so as not just to record but analyze transportation data and make suggestions accordingly. Predictive analytics can provide critical predictions for field service and can be used strategically to position parts and personnel before problems or issues arise. This not only reduces part inventory but ensures overall service quality and reliability (Brown, Basu, & Worth, 2010).

For example, Accenture was interviewed for its multinational presence, and its consequent knowledge of global trade and trends. Accenture has recently collaborated with General Electric on a predictive analytics project (TALERIS) to provide an intelligent operations service for airline carriers around the globe. Another example is health products retailer GNC, which uses a labor management dashboard in distribution centers to track picking completion times and variances, enabling it to shift resources accordingly to keep up with demand. Using data analytics for supply chain management can also optimize shipping. For example,

United Parcel Service (UPS) has been working for a decade on a system called On-Road Integrated Optimization and Navigation that determines the optimal path for road delivery, using big data analytics to handle the data encountered (Noyes, 2014; Rosenbush & Stevens, 2015).

SAP has recently produced a high-performance analytic appliance (HANA) platform that is effectively "live cache" technology. HANA can be used to support an in-memory relational database management system. This technology can dramatically increase the runtime speed of various complex applications in the supply chain and can transform what were once operational tools into decision-making tools. Speed is achieved by virtue of in-core processing and avoiding the need for data aggregation. For example, a materials requirements plan (MRP), which traditionally took hours to run, can now produce results in seconds. Such speed can enable companies to run multiple MRPs to achieve the most desirable scenarios. Another example is in warehouse management, where it is used to support tracking warehouse employees in real time by managing data that tracks the historic movements of employees. Such information can be used to predict task completion times, making labor management more efficient.

The following web link provides additional examples of implementations of data analytics in the supply chain:

SAP HANA—Transforming Business Systems https://www.youtube.com/watch?v = EoPnKSgXzO8

Data warehouse and integration

The amount of data being generated on a daily basis is staggering, and using standard data analytic tools for pulling meaningful data from these enormous data sets is not a practical task. As automation in the supply chain grows, so does the volume of real-time or near-real-time transactional data that is generated from automated systems. This data must be used in conjunction with master (or fixed) data for process execution and monitoring. Big data analytics works mainly with transactional data to provide real-time analytic information that complements the end-to-end visibilities of a supply chain.

Faster and cheaper computer power has accelerated the use of big data warehouse solutions in the supply chain and logistics arena. The drivers for cost-effective data warehousing have been the push for the use of big data and both real-time and predictive analytics. Consequently, data warehouse technologies underpin many of the capabilities offered by the other technologies described in this book. Many of these technologies are attributed to hardware innovations, such as high-capacity RAM, multi-core processor architectures, massive parallel scaling and processing, and large symmetric multiprocessors.

Such innovations have led to the use of an architected data warehouse with in-memory technology as a preferred approach (Imhoff, 2013). An architected approach is more cost effective versus a loosely architected system of components. In-memory technology reduces data processing time, improves flexibility and scalability, and reduces the need for data transformation and aggregation. On the other hand the use of in-memory databases can encounter performance problems when transferring large volumes of data from memory to cache. Thus there needs to be good compatibility between the data warehouse platform and the data analytics software that is performing the querying.

The use of data virtualization with this approach can further reduce the data design effort, data movement, data redundancy, and ultimately costs. It also eliminates integration issues across varying types of data sets. On the other hand, it requires careful system performance management such that response times are not degraded in light of varying kinds of data queries. Virtualization can also help data warehouses with accommodating unstructured data forms, such as documents, video, and images. Such varied formats of data can potentially clutter the data warehouse unnecessarily and require new interfaces on the part of the data warehouse to input and output such data.

The following web links provide some additional perspectives on big data in the supply chain:

Big Data and Supply Chain https://www.youtube.com/watch?v = pHdnDtruCkg

Accenture on Usage of Big Data in Supply Chain https://www.youtube.com/watch?v = Bn9jfoQ5PIw

Sensors and telematics

Remote operation and control has become more popular in supply chain and logistics in order to achieve greater operational visibility. Control center types of operations, while traditionally popular in industries such as pipelines and railroads, have now found their place in other industries, such as retail. Sensor technologies, such as radio frequency identification

(RFID) and telematics, have been recognized recently for their potential in the supply chain area and have capabilities to provide the ability to extend the reach of this control beyond a firm's own supply chain. For example, capabilities, such as end-to-end monitoring of shipments and containers, and event management and alerting, can help control the bull-whip effect. Zebra Technologies is a major player in the RFID scene and was interviewed in this study about how these technologies can have a massive impact on tackling future supply chain visibility issues.

By powering the IoT, these sensors provide insight into patterns and also help with keeping track of a company's assets. For example, one can predict and optimize trip time using sensors. Predicting when shipments will be late allows logistics managers immediately to notify customers, rebook warehouse loaders, or reschedule cross-docking operations. Analyzing data over time allows managers to optimize routes and schedules to reduce travel time, plan cross-dock plans with fewer disconnects and manage which drivers provide the best results by route, season, and time of day.

This solution combines data from sensor, supply chain logistics, weather, traffic, and more and applies machine learning to detect repeatable patterns that managers can use to predict transit times and delays under a variety of circumstances. It presents this information in graphical interfaces that managers can access in seconds from any computer, tablet, or smartphone, enabling them to make decisions whenever they are most useful.

Asset utilization is also better handled using sensor technology. Maximizing freight capacity while minimizing fleet waste is another top concern. Typically this is done by combing through reports that are manually tallied and assembled across many levels of the organization, which is labor intensive and error prone.

On the other hand, sensors provide direct "eyes and ears" when assets are in use and when they are idle. It does this without making human time and effort to record and combine information. Combining sensor data with order information allows logistics managers to view a complete picture of asset utilization. For example, not only can managers see when their vehicles were planned for deliveries, they can also know when the vehicle left the yard, when it was actually moving, and when it arrived inside the delivery location. Managers can also monitor the driving habits of individual drivers. As such, the carrier could use the truck longer prior to leaving without affecting the next delivery time (Haughwot, 2015).

It should be noted that there is such a thing as too much data. Data granularity must be decided upon by companies prior to set up, based on both storage capacity and capability of its analytic operations. In some cases, big data analytics must be employed to handle the data generated by a multitude of sensors in order to capture patterns and make informed business decisions.

Some additional information regarding the use of sensing technology, such as RFID, within supply chains can be found in the following web links:

RFID to Monitor and Track Inventory https://www.youtube.com/watch?v = 4CO14dhRVXM

RFID Inventory Management https://www.youtube.com/watch?v = i5dQxNA6TRM

3D printing

3D printing has a direct impact on the supply chain. The opportunity for on-demand manufacturing and the quick production of more customized products that 3D printing offers can reduce lead time, inventory and waste, warehouse costs, and other inefficiencies, while improving product quality. Though manufacturing in some locations can be low cost, operating a global logistics network, including transportation and other distribution expenses, means huge overhead costs. 3D printing can help reduce these overhead costs by enabling businesses to station local manufacturing centers closer to strategic markets, hence reducing the length and complexity of a supply chain while simultaneously helping to reduce the carbon footprint. Regional manufacturing centers will help with inventory concerns, specifically in terms of highly customized goods for consumers. The cost of customization will be brought down significantly, while the range and scope of customization simultaneously increase.

There has been a recent trend in e-commerce: next-day delivery. 3-D printing can make this more viable, with customers being able to expect highly specialized requests to go through in a matter of hours. With the reduction in transportation and sourcing time, retailers, both online and otherwise, will be able to deliver quality goods exceptionally fast. Moreover, the price of the product itself would go down. These advantages could be extended beyond retail, and 3D printing has found popularity in the aerospace, defense, automotive, health care, and consumer products industries.

The major applications of 3D printing include new product prototyping, small runs of high-value replacement parts, and complex customized products (MHI, 2015). While this technology has much promise in the future, there are very few examples of its implementation today. Current adoption levels of 3D printing are about 10%, but it is expected to change significantly within the next 6 years.

The following web links further discuss 3D printing:

CNN Explains 3D Printing https://www.youtube.com/watch?v = e0rYO5YI7kA

3 D Printing Factory https://www.youtube.com/watch?v = YOpko6P-QT0

Social media

Global supply chains by definition are very large and include a number of vendors, distribution centers, suppliers, buyers, manufacturing plants, and logistics service providers. Social media can be used as a mechanism for collective intelligence about a supply chain by gathering information from a broad base of different sources. This collective intelligence can be used to uncover evolving trends or for better informed decision-making.

For example, identifying "social sentiment" has found its way into supply chain and logistics operations with respect to supplier sourcing. Social sentiment on potential vendors and suppliers can be used to support supplier qualification and performance monitoring. It can also be used to identify product design and a lot of problems. Social networking websites, such as Procurious.com, have sprung up recently, with the express purpose of furthering communications between supply chain professionals, hence allowing for improved visibility.

Social media benefits the supply chain industry in many ways. Companies can enhance communication with customers, generate demand, reduce operating costs, mitigate risk, increase productivity, and enhance marketplace intelligence. If companies aren't participating in social media, they could be at a disadvantage because most of their customers, suppliers, and competitors are. Social media can help companies improve supply chain processes and solve existing problems by accessing the collective insights of supply chain trading partners.

Websites, such as Procurious.com, have been emerging, acting as portals through which supply chain professionals can interact and build stronger relationships. CH Robinson, a leading global third-party logistics

(3PL) provider, launched *TMC Connect*, a social media site specifically offered for supply chain clients to interact. Since the site's launch in December 2009, supply chain executives and related key personnel within their customer community have become active members (CH Robinson, 2010).

The following web links shed some additional light on social media's role in the supply chain:

Social Media in the Supply Chain https://www.youtube.com/watch?v = Da1en_iFcTw

Social Analytics for Retail https://www.youtube.com/watch?v = kQh175Crxbw

Drones

Drone technology has been around for some time now, but its use for commercial purposes is strictly regulated in America. Unmanned aircraft can cost effectively automate what was once cost-intensive manual activities, such as field inspection in remote areas or those that are difficult to access, using aircraft equipped with cameras or RFID transponders. Oil companies are also considering employment of drones for certain operations (MHI, 2015). For example, if there is a pipeline malfunction, it is much easier to send a drone out to scout for the cause or location of the malfunction than sending trucks to check the situation. A firm called PINC Air uses drones to track assets in yards. The drones would be used in conjunction with traditional yard management systems (McCrea, 2015).

Online retailers are also considering drones for cost-effective last-mile access and delivery. By 2020 20% of logistics organizations are likely to exploit drones for use in their operations. For example, Amazon has been trying to add drones to its delivery service, through Prime Air, but has faced resistance from the US Federal Aviation Administration. Amazon has recently been cleared for prototype testing, which opens doors for several companies to introduce this technology in the future. Also, Domino's Pizza has started experiments on drone delivery of pizza.

The following web links provide examples of the use of drones in the supply chain:

Amazon Drone Technology Concerns https://www.youtube.com/watch?v = Le46ERPMlWU

Domino's Flying Drone Delivers Pizza https://www.youtube.com/watch?v = -CYT4PFV_Hs

Automated storage and retrieval systems

Another trend is the increasing use of automated elements in the warehouse. An AS and retrieval system (RS) is an integration of automated equipment and controls that can handle, store, and retrieve materials as needed with high precision, accuracy, and speed. Such systems vary from simple, manually controlled order-picking machines operating in small storage structures to massively large, computer-controlled systems that are totally integrated into a manufacturing and distribution process.

Specifically, AS/RS refers to a variety of computer-controlled methods for automatically storing and retrieving loads to and from defined locations. Within an AS/RS environment, one would find one or more of the following technologies: horizontal carrousels, vertical carrousels, vertical lift modules, and/or fixed aisle (F/A) storage and RSs. F/A systems utilize special storage retrieval machines to perform the work needed to insert, extract, and deliver loads to designated input/output locations.

Since warehouse density tends to vary inversely with the number of different items stored, AS/RSs have been found to provide multifold improvements in warehouse productivity in today's environment where the number and diversity of SKUs are rapidly growing.

The benefits of adopting an AS/RS system are quite evident. For one, they improve the organization of products in a warehouse, also allowing for more storage space due to high-density storage and narrower aisles. They also reduce labor (and associated) costs, while simultaneously improving safety conditions.

Warehouse redesign is an integral part of shifting to an automated system. Mecalux is one such company that provides warehouse solutions, such as design and manufacturing of steel racking and other storage solutions. Bastian Robotics is another company that provides turnkey solutions for companies, including implementations of fast pick-and-place robots for enhanced accuracy and speed.

The following web links provide some additional information on AS/RS and robotics:

Pick-and-Place Robots in the Warehouse https://www.youtube.com/watch?v = 6RKXVefE98w

AS/RS System in Action https://www.youtube.com/watch?v = _i8jGdGwpq4

Kiva Robots https://www.youtube.com/watch?v = 6KRjuuEVEZs

Amazon Warehouse Robots https://www.youtube.com/watch?v = cLVCGEmkJs0

Autonomous vehicles

An automated guided vehicle or automatic guided vehicle (AGV) is a mobile robot, most often used in industrial applications for material-handling purposes around a manufacturing facility or warehouse. There has been a steady increase in usage of AGVs in the past few decades, due to decreasing cost. AGVs are employed across multiple industries, primarily pharmaceutical, chemical, manufacturing, automotive, and warehousing. AGVs follow different navigation models; some follow markers or wires on the floor, some use vision, etc. The selection of a model is done based on current requirements and budget. Currently, laser-based AGVs are in high demand and usage. Recent trends are integration with vision systems/image sensors for a wider range of applications.

Common AGV applications include raw materials handling, work-in-process movement, pallet handling, finished product handling, trailer loading, roll handling, and container handling. As with all automated systems, usage of AGVs leads to labor reduction, improved safety, and inventory control. These benefits lead to decreased overall cost, and a 2-year payback is generally anticipated. Implementation times may vary from 6 months to 1 year, based on requirements and necessity of integration with current systems. Autonomous vehicles have been found to improve productivity for routine operations involving the movement of goods and materials. These improvements include enhanced safety, energy savings, operational efficiency, and increased accuracy and consistency.

AGV Solutions was interviewed for this study. AGV Solutions is a provider of AGVs in the North American market. AGV Solutions offers a complete line of standard and custom AGVs. These AGVs offer payloads from a few pounds to 65 tons, lifting heights up to 36 ft, and the use of many types of navigation, such as laser, vision, contour, wire, magnet, and tape.

AGV Solutions' vehicles are usually integrated with the client's current WMS. Full software support is provided with the control software offered. The onboard control system is developed to be less costly compared to other technologies, without compromising the functionality, flexibility, and quality required, and provides access to the AGV's sensors and other additions.

Caterpillar has also been using autonomous vehicles in mining. In addition, Google and other companies have developed and tested autonomous vehicles for passenger use. The passenger vehicle faces many regulatory challenges and may not be in commercial use for some time.

The following web links provide examples of the use of AGVs:

Customized AGV https://www.youtube.com/watch?v = GZG-fDACZ6g

The Future of Caterpillar's Autonomous Vehicles https://www.miningglobal.com/machinery/video-future-caterpillars-autonomous-vehicles

Google Car Project https://www.youtube.com/watch?v = CqSDWo AhvLU&list = PLcNF6Ihx2JoUoNKe4PxLqEcZMM0QW2yG-

Overall, AGVs have been found to improve productivity for routine operations involving the movement of goods and materials. These improvements include enhanced safety, energy savings, operational efficiency, and increased accuracy and consistency. These vehicles have seen increased usage in material handling in manufacturing and warehouses. By 2030 AGVs are expected to represent approximately 25% of the passenger vehicle population in mature markets.

Electronic shelving

Electronic shelf labeling (ESL) is used by innovative retailers for greater operational efficiency. ESL makes possible automatic price and information labeling of items, and customer engagement in the mobility-driven customer paradigm. The ESLs are controlled using state-of-the-art wireless technology and can optimize processes such as inventory management and self-checkout.

With ESLs, price changes can be made based on consumer preferences or the inventory levels of a specific location. This enables retailers to deploy new advertising and promotional campaigns to stores in seconds or minutes instead of weeks or months. The demand for these systems is increasing, with major retail companies looking at the ESL value proposition. Major vendors of ESL systems include Store Electronic Systems and Pricer.

Compass Marketing Inc., partnering with Panasonic, has been working on Powershelf, a system that replaces the billions of paper price tags with labels that display price electronically, allowing retailers to change prices remotely in minutes. The system, expected to be incorporated with weight sensors, will also help with out-of-stock inventory costs, aid in marketing, and help with overall customer experience.

ESL systems are currently being embraced more in European nations, but the demand in America has also been high and growing. There have been reports of a 100% ROI in 1.5–2 years, with replacement only needed every 5 years (Swedberg, 2009). A conservative 5% implementation of ESL in the US market and 20% implementation in European market values the total market to reach just over € 3 billion by 2020.

The following web links provide additional information on ESL:

ESL Systems https://www.youtube.com/watch?v = 06i7RGhxo10

Graphic Electronic Shelf Labels by SES https://www.youtube.com/watch?v = W9apLYsn2RA

Co-op Denmark Electronic Shelf Labels https://www.youtube.com/watch?v = BkEHNquQm94

Optimization software

While optimization software has been utilized in supply chain and logistics operations for some time now, more standardized off-the-shelf packages have become available. In addition, software packages are becoming more equipped with integration capabilities with other systems, such as Enterprise Resource Planning (ERP) and WMS, as well as field and floor technologies. While traditionally such packages involved a high level of optimization capabilities, they are now featuring more data analytics capabilities. Consequently, this transforms the package into a decision-making analytics tool, and not just a mechanical optimization calculator. The popular areas of applications include inventory management (ordering, picking, sourcing, etc.), transportation management (loading, auditing, payment, etc.), and manufacturing management (contract manufacturing strategies).

Another visible trend is the integration of this software into a supply chain execution technology platform, which represents a collection of logistics software applications, also referred to advanced planning systems. This includes WMS, TMS, labor management systems, supply chain visibility, analytics, and other capabilities. As of today, very few companies have yet to implement this kind of integrated platform, relying on loosely integrated solutions from multiple vendors (Lee, O'Marah, & John, 2012). However, it is envisioned that many firms will be seeking single-vendor suites. Many companies are looking to move from a heterogeneous collection of applications into a well-integrated software platform.

One WMS capability that is highly desired among firms is inventory control (Lee, et al, 2012), followed by a flow of goods management. For TMS systems, freight pay, audit, and routing are considered highly desirable. Tighter integration between these two modules would entail the passing of detailed transportation plans to the WMS for execution, with the WMS issuing exceptions back to the TMS.

The use of optimization packages can amount to potential savings in vehicle routing, load building, and logistics network design by 10% or more (MHI, 2015), with a larger potential reduction in total inventory costs. In addition, these packages can help achieve ROI in load building at 5%–10% and 3%–5% in network design. One company that provides this service is ORTEC, along with other services such as load building and network design solutions.

The web link below details more information about optimization software:

ORTEC Planning Solutions https://www.youtube.com/watch?v=FioMx80fqdU

Blockchain

Blockchain is a technology that is mostly associated with cryptocurrencies, especially Bitcoin. But, blockchain has many potential applications, which are just beginning to be explored. Blockchain is merely a digital ledger that cannot be altered. It can improve the speed of transaction execution and validation across multiple parties. These include digitally validating a transaction that has occurred between two entities and rendering it irrefutable. One application that has been mentioned is the use in the cold chain so that each temperature can be recorded at each step in the chain. Another application that is mentioned in the literature is in international logistics by replacing a mostly paper process. However, the process of transitioning from paper to blockchain seems very formidable (Tirschwell, 2018). More information about blockchain can be found in Chapter 4 of this book. The web link below explains blockchain in more detail.

How Does Blockchain Work? https://www.youtube.com/watch?v=SSo_EIwHSd4

Internet of Things

IoT refers to the connection of devices, objects, and machines to the internet. Drones, AS and RSs, and electronic shelving mentioned previously in this chapter are good examples. There are many other examples concerning location tracking, fleet management, etc. For example, Hub Group of Oak Brook, IL, has GPS devices connected to its fleet of containers. It can tell immediately the location of the containers anywhere in the world. Harrison (2018) provides a variety of applications for supply chain management. One problem with connected devices and machines is the potential for hacking into the systems. Microsoft explains its Microsoft Cloud and IoT in the web link below:

Microsoft Cloudand IoT https://www.youtube.com/watch?v = kkmcfukAn9o

Virtual reality

VR first appeared in video games and the movies. Several firms are trying to utilize this in supply chain management. However, so far VR has only been used for marketing purposes by several companies, including IKEA and Chinese online grocery business Yihaodian. IKEA allows customers to visualize their products to see how color and form matches with other purchases. Yihaodian allows customers to browse and shop in the virtual store before buying (Rawlings, 2017). Related is AR. AR has appeared in the order-picking function in warehouses, as we have discussed previously with regard to Vuzix glasses.

Machine learning

Machine learning is a statistical technique in which computers can improve performance over time in the conduct of a particular task. For example, Gain Systems utilizes machine learning to optimize inventory by SKU at particular locations. There are a variety of algorithms that can be used in the machine learning process. One such algorithm is the artificial neural network that is used to model complex relationships and find data patterns. This algorithm is used by Gains Systems to optimize the amount of inventory carried. More on this in Chapter 5 of this book

Closely related to machine learning is artificial intelligence (AI). AI is a software program that simulates human thought. For example, in 2011, the IBM computer Watson was able to beat two all-time champions in the quiz show Jeopardy. AI is used in Google Translate and many of the personal assistants, such as the Apple Siri and Amazon Echo.

The difference between machine learning and AI are discussed in the video below:

AI and Machine Learning https://www.youtube.com/watch?v = q7bKMHdxtPU

Summary

E-commerce has created high-demand variability and changed demand patterns from what was a once seasonal (or lumpy) pattern to a jagged pattern. This trend, coupled with the growth in the volume and multiplicity of SKUs and the demand for direct shipping, has challenged the traditional supply chain and logistics landscape in several ways. It has created major effects on warehouse management due to the increase in direct shipping demand from the distribution center to the customer and consequently has required traditional pick, pack, and ship operations to be more fluid. Overall, technology enablers that can support improving fulfillment are being sought and can tightly integrate with existing ERP systems.

One of the most important findings from the study has been that technology, irrespective of the field it services, adapts at a tremendous pace. While it is not possible to keep track of every emerging and evolving trend in individual systems while managing other business operations, it is possible to rely on organizations that are designed for this sole purpose. Major multinational corporations have hence been outsourcing their supply chain planning and optimization needs to 3PL service providers so they can focus on other issues. This saves time and research effort for these corporations, while simultaneously improving efficiency as 3PL service providers and vendors are in possession of valuable and current domain-specific knowledge in an area as dynamic as the logistics and supply chain field. Different vendors will cater to different parts of a company's supply chain, while it is up to the firm to integrate these components into a supply chain optimization process.

Future vision

As a result of this study, a current view of the future technology architecture of the supply chain is portrayed in Fig. 2.2. Illustrated are the roles within the supply chain of the component technologies that were studied. To a great extent, many of the component technologies that were studied are gradually being used to automate supporting facilities, such as the plant, warehouse, and distribution centers, as well as transportation vehicles. Integration within many of the support systems is required to enable control and monitoring. Commensurate with this integration is the collection and movement of vast amounts of data across systems and the

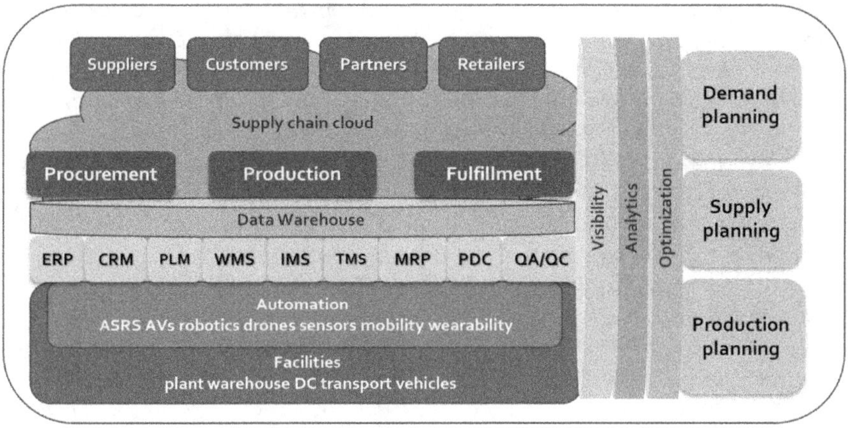

Figure 2.2 Supply Chain Management Future Vision.

ability to store that data in data warehouses for widespread utilization within the firm to support procurement, production, and fulfillment operations. Cloud technology can be viewed as the backplane that enables information collection and sharing with other supply chain stakeholders, such as suppliers, customers, retailers, and other partners. It also makes possible both horizontal and vertical visibility of the supply chain operations. The use of analytics and optimization tools can aid management decision-making capabilities in the areas of demand, supply, production planning, and in other areas as well.

All the technologies described in this chapter work together toward achieving supply chain optimization, reducing overhead costs involved in transportation and storage, improving overall visibility, and consequently allowing for faster response times. For example, consider the following situation:

Company A is a B2C company that receives products from manufacturers and delivers them to the consumer. Company A will clearly have associated warehouse and transportation costs, among others. Company B is one such manufacturer that flies in their product to Company A upon request. To provide better tracking information to the customer, RFID tags could be used, and products could be tracked in real-time. A decision support system could be used for optimized route selection (a product of predictive analytics) based on distance and also on dynamic conditions such as weather. Any change in course by a Company B flight would need to be updated in real-time with Company A, and a cloud-based platform allows for just that. With the updated information, Company A could better coordinate ground transport once the shipment lands. An optimization algorithm could be employed for minimizing time and truck waiting costs as the product is transported to the warehouse operated by Company A.

Once the product enters the warehouse, an automated system will allow AGVs to take over, and transport it to the necessary aisle for storage. To minimize storage space required, and overall warehouse area, the warehouse would be optimally designed and may also be equipped with hi-tech systems such as smart glasses, to enable better warehouse maintenance. The RFID is still in function, and the customer is able to track location information in real time. Once the product is ready to be shipped, an automated warehouse management system would 'talk' to an intelligent pick-and-place robot and update it on visual information of the product that needs to be selected from a pile. The robot's arm, equipped with a 3-D vision system, will be able to successfully sort and pick up the required product. The product would then be loaded onto a truck by an AGV, following packaging, and shipped to the customer. Alternatively, in the near future, drones would automatically latch on to the product and fly it to the customer in time. It must be noted that the customer would be able to track the product in real time, as the RFID tag is still in function until it reaches their doorstep.

A major barrier to adopting new technologies in the supply chain is the lack of a business case to justify investment (MHI, 2015). Here, the major challenge is to cost justify investing in new technologies and capabilities to improve the ability to address the greater variability in customer demand patterns. Fig. 2.2 suggests that a redesigned supply chain network may be required, since cloud computing, used together with analytics, can provide opportunities for greater end-to-end real-time/near-real-time visibility across supply chain partners. Such visibility enables multienterprise and multitier collaboration with supply chain partners while maintaining efficiency and improving performance, and ultimately reducing business and partner risk.

Emerging markets can pose additional barriers for new technology, due to volatile conditions that can complicate growth and production. While companies favor using new technologies in their current market supply chains, companies are not using technology extensively in emerging markets, automating only some essential processes (Degun, 2014). Companies with leading high-performance supply chains tend to use technology more extensively in emerging markets than lower performers do, since leading performers are twice as likely to achieve at least 20% growth in these markets in 2 years.

References

Brown, S., Basu, A., & Worth, T. (2010). Predictive analytics in field service. *Analytics Magazine, November/December.*

Degun, G. (2014). Better use of technology will help emerging market supply chains, says accenture. *Supply Management, September*, 10.

Harrison, M. J. (2018). How IoT in logistics revolutionizes the supply chain management. *Transmetrics Blog, May*. Available from http://transmetrics.eu/blog/iot-logistics-revolutionizes-supply-chain-management/.

Haughwot, J. (2015). Sensor Tech and IoT: Building the intelligent supply chain. Feb 27. http://www.mbtmag.com/articles/2015/02/sensor-tech-and-iot-building-intelligent-supply-chain.

Imhoff, C. (2013). *Architecture matters: Real-time in-memory technologies do not make data warehousing obsolete*. Intelligent Solutions Inc.

Lee, H., O'Marah, K., & John, G. (2012). *The Chief Supply Chain Officer's Report - 2012* (September). SCM World.

Maloney, D. (2015). KPM changes its fulfillment "landscape" with voice. <http://www.dcvelocity.com/articles/20150212-kpm-changes-its-fulfillment-landscape-with-voice> Accessed 6.22.15.

McCrea, B. (2015). Supply chain and logistics technology: YMS takes flight. *Logistics Management*, April 1.

McKeefry, H. L. (2014). Collaborative sourcing reduces costs & time. *EBN, October 2*. 2014, www.ebnonline.com.

MHI. (2015). Supply chain innovation – making the impossible possible. *MHI Industry Report*, April 6.

Noosh, Inc. (2014). 2014 Project & Procurement Management Benchmark Report.

Noyes, K. (2014). The shortest distance between two points? At UPS, it's complicated. *Fortune, July 25*. Available from www.fortune.com.

Phillips, A. (2015). Mobility, collaboration and transportation: key supply chain trends for 2015. <http://www.supplychaindigital.com/supplychainmanagement/3745/Mobility-collaboration-and-transportation:-key-supply-chain-trends-for-2015/>.

Rawlings, C. (2017). *VR and AR: A game changer in retail and supply chain?* (April 19). KPMG. Available from https://home.kpmg.com/sg/en/home/media/press-contributions/2017/04/vr-and-ar-a-game-changer-in-retail-and-supply-chain.html.

Robinson, C.H. (2010). Press release, "TMC's new social media site has supply chain executives talking — to each other." February 10. <http://www.chrobinson.com/en/us/About-Us/Newsroom/Press-Releases/2010/TMCs-new-social-media-site/>.

Rosenbush, S., & Stevens, L. (2015). At UPS, the algorithm is the driver. *Wall Street Journal, February 16*.

Swedberg, C. (2009). Two food chains trial RFID-based electronic shelf labels. March 30. <http://www.rfidjournal.com/articles/view?4737/>.

Tirschwell, Peter (2018). Blockchain theory's path to reality in shipping beset by details and distrust. *Journal of Commerce*. Online, May 16. https://www.joc.com/technology/blockchain-theorys-path-reality-shipping-beset-details-and-distrust_20180516.html.

Titze, C., & Barger, R. (2015). Evolving concepts in the supply chain. *Gartner Report*, January 19.

You Tube Videos

Moving Supply Chain to the Cloud https://www.youtube.com/watch?v = ae_DKNwK_ms

MCL Enterprise Mobility Platform https://www.youtube.com/watch?v = wSis03cW9II

Future of Mobility in Supply Chain https://www.youtube.com/watch?v = WcXWo2zT2bs

Future of Field Service https://www.youtube.com/watch?v=UlpGDrSmg38

SAP HANA – Transforming Business Systems https://www.youtube.com/watch?v=EoPnKSgXzO8

Big Data and Supply Chain https://www.youtube.com/watch?v=pHdnDtruCkg

Accenture on Usage of Big Data in Supply Chain https://www.youtube.com/watch?v=Bn9jfoQ5PIw

RFID to Monitor and Track Inventory https://www.youtube.com/watch?v=4CO14dhRVXM

RFID Inventory Management https://www.youtube.com/watch?v=i5dQxNA6TRM

CNN Explains 3D Printing https://www.youtube.com/watch?v=e0rYO5YI7kA

3 D Printing Factory https://www.youtube.com/watch?v=YOpko6P-QT0

Social Media in the Supply Chain https://www.youtube.com/watch?v=Da1en_iFcTw

Social Analytics for Retail https://www.youtube.com/watch?v=kQh175Crxbw

Amazon Drone Technology Concerns https://www.youtube.com/watch?v=Le46ERPMlWU

Domino's Flying Drone Delivers Pizza https://www.youtube.com/watch?v=-CYT4PFV_Hs

Pick-and-Place Robots in the Warehouse https://www.youtube.com/watch?v=6RKXVefE98w

AS/RS System in Action https://www.youtube.com/watch?v=_i8jGdGwpq4

Kiva Robots https://www.youtube.com/watch?v=6KRjuuEVEZs

Amazon Warehouse Robots https://www.youtube.com/watch?v=cLVCGEmkJs0

Customized AGV https://www.youtube.com/watch?v=GZG-fDACZ6g

The Future of Caterpillar's Autonomous Vehicles https://www.mininngglobal.com/machinery/video-future-caterpillars-autonomous-vehicles

Google Car Project https://www.youtube.com/watch?v=CqSDWoAhvLU&list=PLcNF6Ihx2JoUoNKe4PxLqEcZMM0QW2yG-

ESL Systems https://www.youtube.com/watch?v=06i7RGhxo10

Graphic Electronic Shelf Labels by SES https://www.youtube.com/watch?v=W9apLYsn2RA

Co-op Denmark Electronic Shelf Labels https://www.youtube.com/watch?v = BkEHNquQm94

ORTEC Planning Solutions https://www.youtube.com/watch?v = FioMx80fqdU

How Does Blockchain Work? https://www.youtube.com/watch?v = SSo_EIwHSd4

Microsoft Cloud and IoT https://www.youtube.com/watch?v = kkmcfukAn9o

AI and Machine Learning https://www.youtube.com/watch?v = q7bKMHdxtPU

CHAPTER 3

Impact of exponential technologies on global supply chain management

Unsal Ozdogru
Department of Information and Decision Sciences, The University of Illinois at Chicago, Chicago, IL, United States

Contents

Introduction

Rapid technological advances over the last several decades have significantly impacted all areas of industries, such as communication, energy, food and beverage, transportation, education, health, and manufacturing, among many others. The leading exponential technologies, including but

Technology in Supply Chain Management and Logistics
DOI: https://doi.org/10.1016/B978-0-12-815956-9.00003-X

not limited to blockchain, Internet of Things (IoT), machine learning, virtual/augmented/extended reality (VR/AR/ER), 3D printing, big data, and robotics have the potential to influence supply chains globally. As a result, supply chain performance for most companies has become highly correlated with the combination of technologies adopted within their operations.

This chapter will provide a literature survey of the exponential technologies used in global supply chain management and elaborate adoption profiles for each as a reference base to guide enterprises' decision-making efforts with regard to early investment, procurement, and implementation of these technologies. Our first objective is to identify the leading exponential technologies. Second, we want to understand the implications of these technologies in terms of their potential value. Then, we will identify the most fertile areas for effective deployment of the technology within supply chain operations, focusing on the following characteristics:

- service architecture identifying the underlying layers of systems and information necessary for deployment and
- adoption parameters that decision-makers will utilize to justify investment in the technology. The general areas may include:
    - Required operational transaction density.
    - The potential for reducing information uncertainty.
    - Improved operational efficiency.
    - Improved supply chain visibility.
    - Scalability and migration path of the technology.
    - Realization timeframe from ramp-up to on-board.
    - Improved utilization of operational information and data.
    - Network effects in terms of the degree of indispensability that can be achieved.
    - Impacts on the supply chain network topology and the degree of self-organization and customization that can be enabled.
    - The ability to align with enterprise strategy and business goals.
- Ease of integration with legacy systems and interoperability.
- Use cases depicting scenarios for provisional deployment and proofs of concept.
- Risks identifying the challenges, caveats, pitfalls, complexity, costs, and exit criteria.
- Cross-integration and dependency with other exponential technologies and/or emerging technologies.

Literature review

A firm's supply chain is typically one of the foremost functional areas where technological change is first applied, since supply chain costs may comprise up to 80% of sales depending on the industry (Sehgal, 2010). Global supply chains are complex and face a variety of risks (BCI, 2017; Manuj & Mentzer, 2011). Risk arises in sourcing, delivery speed, costs, and quality (Brosch, 2015; Morales, 2015).

Rapid advances in technology have created many opportunities in every industry for companies to cross borders and expand their business to gain competitive advantages while minimizing risks and ultimately increase their profit (Degun, 2014; Myerson, 2016; Robinson, 2018). Technology and big data can be leveraged to overcome the skills and resources gap that hampers effective tracking (BCI, 2017); and, it can not only increase the tractability and traceability of the products on the global supply chains (Groenfeldt, 2017; Popper & Lohr, 2017; Yiannas, 2017), but also improve the integrity of these supply chains (Bindi, 2017). Consequently, supply chains must continuously adapt to technological advancements within their operations and systems to contribute to the health of their respective enterprises (Mariani, Quasney, & Raynor, 2015; Myersen, 2018; Robinson, 2018; Slone, Dittmann, & Mentzer, 2010). Adapting the technologies helps companies to increase their competition (Alleven, 2017; Marr, 2017).

Liotine, Pagano, and Varma (2016) analyzed the technological trends in logistics and supply chain management in the United States that are being followed by 10 corporations. The study revealed attributes and criteria exhibited by companies with regard to implementation of maturing, growth, and emerging technologies all within the supply chain. A key finding of the study was that the technologies, regardless of their place in the technology adoption life cycle, exhibited a rapid rate of change of evolution from early instability into maturity. They also reflected the law of accelerating returns with regards to the assurance of benefits such as cost reduction, improved customer response and increased process efficiency, ultimately breeding new operational ecosystems within their firms.

Several new technologies including information technology, the IoT, big data, the cloud, 3D printing, blockchain, artificial intelligence (AI) could have profound exponential effects on supply global chains (Columbus, L., 2016; Ernst & Young, 2016; Haughwot, 2015; Kadiyala, 2018; Lanng, 2015; Lechmacher, 2016; Min, 2010, 2016; O'Byrne, 2018;

O'Marah, 2017; Rosenberg, 2016). While some of these technologies seem like solutions in search of a problem, they promise benefits potentially greater than the technologies that supply chains are currently adapting (Buntz, 2017). They represent advances that are expected to create significantly positive, nonlinear economic benefits for the companies that produce or use them (Casey & Wong, 2017; Morningstar, 2016).

Within the supply chain, exponential technologies will require applications, development effort, and a corporate dynamism such that their performance matures to higher steady-state levels (Cann, 2016). For companies in managing a wide network of partners, blockchain provides a path to access accurate information in real time with high transparency. Kim and Chai (2017) applied diffusion of innovation theory to explain how supplier innovativeness has diffused into the supply chain and how global sourcing moderates the relationship among supplier innovativeness, information sharing, strategic sourcing, and supply chain agility. Banerjee (2018) provided a high level of understanding of how blockchain, as a decentralized platform, can complement ERP technologies in all supply chain functions, bringing in transparency, visibility, efficiency, and cost reduction. Distributed ledger technology (the blockchain) together with the GS1 standard to create a permissioned, fully distributed network of peers to share data in a standard, secure, transparent, and robust way (Collak, 2018; Margo, 2017). Wolfson (2018) articulated how various blockchains connect participants through a transparent, permanent, and shared record of food origin details, processing data, shipping details, and more. Integrating and adopting blockchain technology help reduce costs, increase traceability, and enhance security.

Vollmer (2018) and Columbus (2017) observe that the IoT is playing a significant role in today's supply chain, and advanced analytics-driven data aggregation platforms are now earmarked as an area to watch. Newman (2018) emphasized that the IoT is set to revolutionize the supply chain with both operational efficiencies (asset tracking, vendor relations, forecasting, inventory, connected fleets, scheduled maintenance) and revenue opportunities made possible with just this type of transparency. For the IoT to be truly effective, all members of one's global supply chain must be connected.

New knowledge and insights from machine learning can be used to find the core set of factors, influencing such as, but not limited to, inventory levels, demand forecasting, etc., with the greatest predictive accuracy (Columbus, 2018). Using emerging technology instead of past methods could be more efficient and accurate, saving businesses time and money (Krauth, 2018). Kshetri (2018) used multiple cases and illustrated how supply chain management objectives, such as cost, quality, speed, dependability, risk reduction, sustainability, and flexibility, can be achieved using blockchain technology.

Identification and implications of exponential technologies in global supply chain

The survey report (MHI & Deloitte, 2018) from more than 1100 respondents across a wide range of industries featured in-depth profiles of the five next-generation innovations, robotics and automation, big data and predictive analytics, IoT/sensors, AI, and driverless vehicles/drones as having the greatest impact on global supply chains. Other technologies highlighted were wearable and mobile technology, inventory and network optimization, sensors and automatic identification, cloud computing and storage, 3D printing, and blockchain. The respondents believed that many of these technologies have the potential to disrupt the status quo and create a lasting competitive advantage for companies that adopt them. These technologies can work together to create operational efficiencies and harness digital supply chain data that can lead to significant improvements in visibility, agility, and responsiveness to customer demands. Barriers to adoption of these technologies include a clear business case to justify the investment, understanding of technology landscape along with the effects on their business, access to capital to make investments, adequate talent to effectively implement along with utilization of the technology, and cultural aversion to risk, which means they are waiting until technology is fully proven and established. The top five of these technologies (MHI & Deloitte, 2018) are given in Table 3.1 with current disruption or competitive advantage, 5-year adoption rates and their implications.

Accenture surveyed supply chain leaders across 12 industries and seven geographies to discover how they are embracing new technologies, such as big data analytics, AI with techniques like machine learning (including deep learning), blockchain, 3D printing, and robotics, which can help manage supply chain complexity, accelerate responsiveness, and response time to market. The tendency in almost all industries to combine IoT technologies with either big data analytics or machine/deep learning and/or security indicated the strength of interest in turning the supply chain into a platform of networked value creation (Schulman, Hajibashi, & Narsalay, 2018).

Accenture, in collaboration with the Technology Vision, surveyed 6300 + executives from 25 countries Five trends shaping the way

Table 3.1 Survey results for top five technologies by MHI industry report 2018.

	Current disruption or competitive advantage (%)	Implications	5-Year projected adoption rates (%)
Robotics and Automation	65	Increase in productivity, efficiency, order fulfillment rate, order delivery	73
Predictive Analytics	62	Increase in traceability, visibility, forecasting, and customer and vendor relationship management, efficiency, job performance	82
IoT	59	Increase in efficiency, speed, throughput, quality	79
AI	53	flexibility, reliability, speed, productivity, accuracy, and reduce in product losses	47
Driverless Vehicles and Drones	52	Improving accuracy, efficiencies, and reducing costs and aligning costs to business strategy, improving service quality, and conserving human capital	50

technology is increasing businesses' impact on companies, government agencies, and other organizations are AI, ER, data veracity, frictionless business, and IoT (Accenture & TechVision, 2018; Bonn, 2017). DHL has 15% improvement on the average in productivity while achieving higher accuracy rates using ER solutions (Milnes, 2017). L'Oréal's Beauty Lab cut down the launch time of products from months to weeks by testing design, branding, and packaging in VR, speeding decision-making, and reducing risks

In a Gartner survey, it was reported that 65% of the supply chain professionals think that adopting and investing in technologies, such as autonomous mobile robots, AI, blockchains, and virtual assistance, gives companies a competitive edge (Beadle, 2017). Companies such as Walmart, Maersk, UPS, FedEx, and British Airways have been experimenting with blockchain technology to improve their efficiency and accuracy (Krauth, 2018). In addition, use cases from the other companies—Provenance, Alibaba, Lockheed Martin, Chronicle, Everledger, and Gemalto, among others—have shown that supply chain objectives, such as minimizing cost and risk, increasing quality, speed, dependability, sustainability, and flexibility, can be achieved to improve supply chain performance, trust, and security for all parties involved in the process (Kshetri, 2018).

Technology adoption

Supply chain leaders are expected to embrace new technologies continuously to differentiate themselves from their competition. Adopting the right combination of supply chain innovations with many dynamic parts together into a single seamless framework that can drive effective decision-making is a complex and challenging process. (Eshkenazi, 2018; Laaper, Yauch, Wellener, & Robinson, 2018) Adoption of new technologies will require the integration of data and information from multiple sources. To drive AI, robotics, AR, ER, sensors, blockchain, cloud computing, big data, predictive analytics, and other revolutionary technologies to their full potential, companies must make a significant effort in their business processes and strategies, infrastructure, and hardware considerations. This may even require companies to reshape their supply chains into digital supply networks.

Digital supply chain networks help companies speed up their decision-making, respond better with changing market needs, reduce risk, increase internal/external transparency, and, as a result, increase top and bottom lines (consisting of reducing operating costs, improving product quality, increasing visibility and sales effectiveness, generating new business development opportunities, and creating strategic advantages), which all help boost their profitability. As a result, many organizations have started the ascent to digitalization then to intelligent modern supply chains. As supply chains rapidly digitized and disrupted, all supply chain links in the future will ultimately be connected, and information will be shared seamlessly across all interested parties.

To help manufacturing firms think about their digital options, Srai (2018) developed a series of scenarios for their supply chains, including automated e-sourcing of parts and digitally enabled production processes through smart factory design and automation to direct-to-the customer e-commerce, real-time monitoring, and perpetual self-optimization, among others (CISCO, 2018). Digitization has enabled Cisco's supply chain to become more efficient and aligned while improving visibility. Its efforts together with digitalization have increased productivity by 35% and saved 40% on capital expenditures. Cisco has enhanced visibility to its material supplies from once a week to four times a week and improved its ability to meet customer delivery commitments by 5%—10% in terms of scheduled lead time. Among others, digital supply solutions use AI and IoT technologies and helped customers like Microsoft with $200M in inventory reduction, Lennox with 90% less time needed for data collection, and increased Komplett Group's supply chain efficiency by 28% higher (SAP, 2018).

Supply chain complexity has been pushing companies to explore blockchain to improve food tracking, safety, and supply chain transparency (Accenture & TechVision, 2018). Large competitors like Nestlé, Unilever, Tyson, Kroger, and Walmart and others are partnering with IBM to develop a blockchain that will allow better transparency and tracking of food movement across their complex supply chains. By using blockchain, any enterprise with a vast logistics network can identify sources of potential risks, such as contaminated produce, defective parts, and fraudulent vendors. It helps companies react ultimately to enhancing operational speed while protecting the public and mitigating corporate risk. AT&T (2017) shared survey results about IoT and its adoption within the manufacturing, transportation, and supply chain. The top reasons to utilize IoT are an increase in visibility, better response time and delivery, greater asset utilization, improved operational efficiency, enhanced customer experience, risk mitigation, and quality assurance. For long-term success, AT&T highlights that organizations need a provider that can help design an IoT system that is scalable, flexible, and highly secure; companies look for six critical factors when selecting their IoT platform provider: track record, ecosystem, global footprint, multinetwork, adapt and scale, and hybrid cloud environments.

Oracle (2016) conducted a survey of leaders across North America, Europe, the Middle East and Africa, Central and South America, and Asia-Pacific. It found that companies are ready to adopt cloud-based supply chain management (SCM) processes but need to see concrete evidence of business benefits and want both full vendor support and end-to-end solutions. The top three advantages receiving significant responses for cloud-based supply chain management are faster implementation (61%), cost savings (60%), and improved customer service (59%). Security was one of the other top concerns. It is projected that product life cycle management is expected to experience the most growth in cloud-based SCM over the next 2 years, followed by logistics, global trade, and ideation and innovation.

During the last decade, enterprises were inclined to build or leverage custom and specialized hardware rather than the typical "one-size-fits-all-tasks" approach. This shift has enabled the greater processing speeds that drive integrated and sophisticated experiences at the edge. Instead of doubling its data center footprint, Google built a computer chip—the tensor processing unit—specifically to run deep neural networks that outperform standard processors by 30–80 times in efficiency. It is among a host of new, specialized processing units that Facebook, Microsoft, Amazon, Baidu, and other leading firms are using to train and run AI models. For businesses looking to lead in intelligent environments, both custom and accelerated hardware options are a key element of the path to real-time insights and action (Accenture & TechVision, 2018). Table 3.2 provides several successful examples of adoption across various technologies.

Technology providers

Based on our literature and survey of technologies that have been impacting global supply chain management, we focus on cloud, IoT, AI/ML, and blockchain with the leading providers all having PaaS, IaaS, and SaaS platforms.

Amazon

Amazon Web Services (AWS) offer industrial IoT (IIoT) and blockchain solutions to help customers optimize industrial operations and increase productivity and efficiency. IIoT bridges the gap between legacy industrial

Table 3.2 Examples of technology implications.

Company	Technology	Facts from adoptions
GE	AR	Improving worker productivity in wiring wind turbines by 34%
DHL	XR	Providing visual displays of order picking and placement direction, freeing operators' hands of paper instructions and allowing them to work more efficiently and comfortably, 15% productivity improvements while achieving higher accuracy rates
L'Oréal	VR	Cut down the launch time of products from months to weeks by testing design, branding, and packaging, speeding decision-making, and reducing risks
NY's Icahn School of Medicine at Mt. Sinai	AI (Deep Patient)	Armed with an analysis of electronic health records from 700,000 patients, Deep Patient taught itself to predict risk factors for 78 different diseases
Walmart	Blockchain	Reduced the time it took to trace in-transit mangoes back to their source of origin from 6 days to 2.2 seconds
Kemppi	IoT	Brought its IoT solution to market faster and saves 50% on development costs
Centratech	IoT	Increased productivity of field technicians by 50%
Siemens	IoT	Went project from conception to full production in less than 8 weeks

Source: Retrieved from Accenture & TechVision. (2018). *Redefine your company based on the company you keep: Intelligent enterprise unleashed.* Accenture. Retrieved from https://www.accenture.com/t20180227T215953Z__w__/us-en/_acnmedia/Accenture/next-gen-7/tech-vision-2018/pdf/Accenture-TechVision-2018-Tech-Trends-Report.pdf; Amazon. (2018). *AWS.* Retrieved from https://aws.amazon.com/partners/blockchain/.

equipment and infrastructure, and new technologies such as machine learning, cloud, mobile, and edge computing. Customers use IIoT applications for predictive quality and maintenance and remotely to monitor their operations from anywhere. AWS gives customers access to flexible and cost-effective resources to deploy quickly and experiment with blockchain networks in minutes and to pay only for what they use (Amazon, 2018).

Cisco

The Cisco blockchain framework details the necessary elements for a simple, secure, scalable enterprise-grade blockchain that is based on Cisco's propriety technology. Its blockchain framework is composed of four reference groups: platform, interfaces, infrastructure, and network and security and analytics (Cisco, 2018).

Communication and information are crucial to an efficient supply chain. Securely extending access and visibility throughout the supply chain can create an integrated workflow that promotes innovation, improves efficiency, facilitates collaboration, and decreases business risk. Cisco Connected Manufacturing helps information and decisions flow quickly through the supply chain and organization. Companies can respond immediately to evolving market demands. The result is greater control, lower costs, increased responsiveness, and better business decisions.

IBM

IBM Supply Chain Insights has AI capabilities to help customers cut through data noise and get the insights needed to act faster, with confidence. It enables customers to predict, quickly assess, and more effectively mitigate disruptions and risks to optimize supply chain decision-making and performance. Key features of IBM Supply Chain Insights are AI for Supply Chain, Fast Start Program, Open Integration Platform, and Security and Privacy in the Cloud (IBM, 2018).

IBM Food Trust™ is a collaborative network of growers, processors, wholesalers, distributors, manufacturers, retailers, and others to enhance visibility and accountability in each step of the food supply. Powered by the IBM Blockchain Platform, IBM Food Trust directly connects participants through a permissioned, permanent, and shared record of food origin details, processing data, shipping details, and more.

Intel

Connected logistics technology from Intel powers a fully integrated supply chain solution that provides shippers with a granular view of shipments at the pallet, package, and even item level. Intel's supply chain solution can be customized for monitoring shipment-critical variables and can easily be integrated with climate control and freight-tracking technology. Moreover, it can be used to help analyze and optimize a company's entire supply chain efficiency (Intel, 2018).

Microsoft

Microsoft Azure is an ever-expanding set of cloud services to help organizations meet their business challenges. It is the freedom to build, manage, and deploy applications on a massive, global network using their favorite tools and framework. Azure uses a variety of technologies, such as IoT, blockchain, AI, big data, and analytics, among others to bring solutions to the companies including, but not limited to, manufacturing, retail, and government. Azure for Manufacturing helps to keep up with customers' needs and drives business transformation by modernizing to a smart factory. Through the IIoT and Microsoft Azure, companies gain actionable insights and respond quickly to customer feedback and market trends. Azure for retail creates a personalized and seamless shopping experience that influences buying behavior, empowers employees to delight consumers with outstanding service at every point along their shopping journey and optimize retail operations with an intelligent, trusted, and secure platform (Microsoft, 2018).

Oracle

Cloud technology, for a lower cost and with minimal risk, enables the transformation of a supply chain into a digital and scalable solution—integrated and ready for the connected marketplace. With improved inventory visibility, businesses can spot opportunities for growth and profit, and then take full advantage of them quickly, securely, and cost-effectively. Cloud SCM also enables businesses to access intelligent data and predictive analytics from the IoT. Extending these capabilities to employees and business partners makes everyone more efficient, accurate, and collaborative in their work—helping them deliver better business results. Benefits are visibility, agility, lower operational cost, improved collaboration, ease of use, and security. A complete, fully converged, integrated suite of cloud-based supply chain management solutions consists of the following components: logistics, product life cycle management, supply chain planning, procurement, order management, manufacturing, maintenance, and IoT applications (Oracle, 2018).

SAP

SAP Integrated Business Planning is a real-time cloud-based solution that combines capabilities for sales and operations; demand, response, and supply planning; and inventory optimization, powered by in-memory computing technology within SAP HANA, to meet demand rapidly and profitably (SAP, 2018).

Barriers, challenges, and limitations

Challenges exist in every stage of all business processes. The top 12 challenges in supply chains from the MHI and Deloitte (2018) survey results are:

- food safety;
- spoilage and contamination;
- visibility of inbound and outbound shipments;
- implementing sustainability programs;
- out-of-stock situations;
- omnichannel fulfillment;
- insight into supply and demand;
- synchronization of the supply chain;
- insight into customer behavior and product usage;
- increasing competitive intensity;
- rising customer expectations;
- forecasting;
- hiring qualified workers; and
- customer demands on supply.

With rapid advancements over the last few decades, the leading exponential technologies have been influencing supply chains globally to help overcome these challenges. Companies that are already using, expanding, or considering these new technologies for adoption in their supply chain operations are impacting many of the above challenges.

According to the MHI and Deloitte (2018) survey, three main barriers to adoption of supply chain innovations are lack of clear business case and return on investment, lack of adequate skills and workforce, and trust-building and cybersecurity in digital. These three barriers are increased by a lack of understanding of the technology landscape and the lack of access to capital to make investments. Barriers to the top 5 exponential technologies are summarized in Table 3.3.

Key concerns in adopting IoT technology include selecting the right solutions, up-front costs, security concerns, and implementation costs (AT&T, 2017). While sophisticated, smart, connected devices are an integral part of IoT (Lehmacher, Betti, Beecher, Grotemeier, & Lorenzen, 2017), they are also prone to cyber risk that exerts pressure on both

Table 3.3 Barriers to adoption for top five technologies.

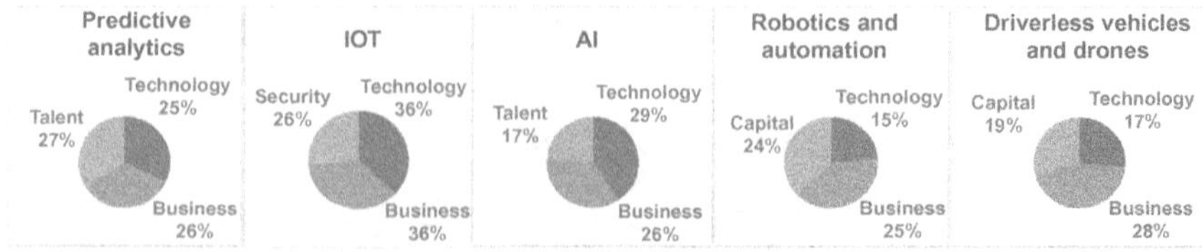

Source: Adapted from MHI & Deloitte (2018). *The 2018 MHI annual industry report—Overcoming barriers to NextGen supply chain innovation.* Retrieved from https://www.mhi.org/publications/report.

government and business leaders to implement appropriate security and privacy policies across organizations, manufacturing networks, and supply chains.

The top challenges in adopting cloud-based SCM solutions are security, which is the biggest challenge at 49%, followed closely by concerns over both IT and business disruption at 42%, lack of enough expertise at 38%, and a shortage of internal skills/expertise at 36% (Oracle, 2016).

Despite the high potential benefits and expectations in global supply chains, blockchain-based solutions have several major challenges and drawbacks that must be addressed (Kshetri, 2018; Casey & Wong, 2017). Global supply chain operates in a complex environment that requires various parties to comply with diverse laws, customs, and regulations. Lack of fully complying with all these produces a risky environment. Another challenge is to create blockchain that is seamlessly able to address fraudulent and manipulative activities. Implementation of blockchain involves bringing all the relevant parties together, which is hard to attain, in particular, if some supply chain partners do not have a high degree of computerization.

Companies compete through strategic partnerships and can expand partner networks faster when partnerships are technology-based. Thus outdated business systems will be major hindrances to growth (Accenture & TechVision, 2018). According to the study by Barkus (2017), regulatory control or lack of universal partner acceptance will be the biggest barriers to adoption. However, there are also a few technological challenges that need to be addressed to support enterprise requirements, including scalability, confidentiality and security, and integration/flexibility. Banerjee (2018) summarizes the key challenges in adopting blockchain for supply chains as infrastructure and network, interoperability, costs of on-boarding and maintenance, data storage cost on blockchain (data per transaction), data validation latency, payload size restriction, regulatory and legal acceptance, and trust.

Despite the potential challenges and risks around security and privacy, companies need to adopt new technologies as an opportunity to increase value across their supply chain operations. Companies that embrace new technologies, adopt early, anticipate challenges, and deal with them strategically to overcome all barriers are most likely to be successful.

Summary

Using a variety of resources, including research citations, third-party information, and case studies, we have collected detailed information on technologies that impact global supply chains. The information acquired from these resources is organized and synthesized. We found out that technologies such as robotics, AI, IoT, VR/AR/ER, big data, and blockchain, among others, are transforming businesses across various industries and sectors, and disruption is expected to accelerate. Depending on the technology and business strategy, the impact could be in one or more areas such as to increase traceability, speed, flexibility, reliability, visibility, efficiency, job performance, order fulfilment rate, and order delivery; to improve accuracy, productivity, service quality, customer, and vendor relationships; and to reduce costs and align costs to business strategy.

Business leaders need closely to understand potential transformations and disruptions in the entire world of supply chain (Accenture & TechVision, 2018). It is noted that the collaborative efforts of industry leaders worldwide demonstrate that technology is at the root of partnerships. Combined adoptions of technologies such as AI, robotics, IoT, 3D printing, AR/VR/XR, and blockchain could also have a tremendous impact on the supply chains (Banerjee, 2018).

Acknowledgments

First, I would like to express my sincere appreciation, and send my special thanks to Prof. Tony Pagano for encouraging me to contribute to this book and for being the technical reviewer of my work. I am also thankful to Prof. Matt Liotine for providing me with his vision, comments, and suggestions. Last, but not least, I am deeply grateful to my daughter Larissa and my entire family in Istanbul for their unconditional support, patience, and understanding that I needed during the course of putting this study together.

References

Accenture., & TechVision. (2018). *Redefine your company based on the company you keep: Intelligent enterprise unleashed*. Accenture. Retrieved from https://www.accenture.com/t20180227T215953Z__w__/us-en/_acnmedia/Accenture/next-gen-7/tech-vision-2018/pdf/Accenture-TechVision-2018-Tech-Trends-Report.pdf.

Alleven, M. (2017, May 5). Walmart looks to take on Amazon in the IoT. *Fiercewireless*. Retrieved from https://www.fiercewireless.com/wireless/walmart-looks-to-take-amazon-iot.

Amazon. (2018). *AWS*. Retrieved from https://aws.amazon.com/partners/blockchain/.

AT&T. (2017). *AT&T Business*. Retrieved from AT&T: https://www.business.att.com/content/productbrochures/the-tech-race-and-iot-brief.pdf.

Banerjee, A. (2018). Blockchain technology: Supply chain insights from ERP. *Advances in Computers*. Available from https://doi.org/10.1016/bs.adcom.2018.03.007.

Barkus, J. (2017). Will blockchain for supply chain change everything? *Manufacturing Leadership/Council*. Retrieved from <https://www.manufacturingleadershipcouncil.com/2017/10/26/will-blockchain-supply-chain-change-everything/>.

BCI. (2017). *BCI supply chain resilience report 2017*. Retrieved from https://www.risk-methods.net/resources/research/BCI-Resilience-Report-2017.pdf.

Beadle, J. (2017, December 21). Gartner predictions for the future of supply chain operations in 2018. *Supply chain*. Retrieved from https://www.gartner.com/smarterwithgartner/gartner-predictions-for-the-future-of-supply-chain-operations-in-2018/.

Bindi, T. (2017, March 24). Alibaba and AusPost team up to tackle food fraud with blockchain. *ZDNET*. Retrieved from https://www.zdnet.com/article/alibaba-and-auspost-team-up-to-tackle-food-fraud-with-blockchain/.

Bonn. (2017, August 2). *DHL supply chain makes smart glasses new standard in logistics*. Retrieved from DHL: www.dhl.com/en/press/releases/releases_2017/all/logistics/dhl_supply_chain_makes_smart_glasses_new_standard_in_logistics.

Brosch, A. (2015, July 27). 6 Global supply chain challenges to ignore at your own risk. *InBoundLogistics*. Retrieved from http://www.inboundlogistics.com/cms/article/6-global-supply-chain-challenges-to-ignore-at-your-own-risk/.

Buntz, B. (2017). *The ordinary magic of the 21st century supply chain*. Internet of Things Institute. Retrieved from http://www.ioti.com/industrial-iot/ordinary-magic-21st-century-supply-chain.

Cann, O. (2016, June 23). These are the top 10 emerging technologies of 2016. *World Economic Forum*. Retrieved from https://www.weforum.org/agenda/2016/06/top-10-emerging-technologies-2016/.

Casey, M. J., & Wong, P. (2017, March 3). Global supply chains are about to get better thanks to blockchain. *Harvard Business Review*. Retrieved from https://hbr.org/2017/03/global-supply-chains-are-about-to-get-better-thanks-to-blockchain.

CISCO. (2018). Retrieved from https://www.cisco.com/c/dam/en/us/solutions/collateral/digital-transformation/supply-chain-digital-age.pdf?dtid = osscdc000283.

Collak, V. (2018, May 22). Blockchain in supply chain—How to use the distributed ledger to trace products. *Forbes*. Retrieved from https://www.forbes.com/sites/forbestechcouncil/2018/05/22/blockchain-in-supply-chain-how-to-use-the-distributed-ledger-to-trace-products/.

Columbus, L. (2016, September 25). Forrester's top 15 emerging technologies to watch, 2017–2021. *Forbes*. Retrieved from https://www.forbes.com/sites/louiscolumbus/2016/09/25/forresters-top-15-emerging-technologies-to-watch-2017-2021.

Columbus, L. (2017, March 19). Retrieved from https://www.forbes.com/sites/louiscolumbus/2017/03/19/internet-of-things-will-revolutionize-retail.

Columbus, L. (2018, June 11). Retrieved from https://www.forbes.com/sites/louiscolumbus/2018/06/11/10-ways-machine-learning-is-revolutionizing-supply-chain-management/.

Degun, G. (2014). Better use of technology will help emerging market supply chains, says Accenture. *Supply Chain Management.* Retrieved from CIPS: https://www.cips.org/supply-management/news/2014/september/better-use-of-technology-will-help-emerging-market-supply-chains-says-accenture/.

Ernst & Young. (2016). *Digital supply chain: It's all about that data.*

Eshkenazi, A. (2018, April 6). Transitioning to digital supply networks. *APICS.* Retrieved from http://www.apics.org/sites/apics-blog/think-supply-chain-landing-page/thinking-supply-chain/2018/04/06/supply-chains-to-digital-supply-networks.

Groenfeldt, T. (2017, March 5). IBM and Maersk apply blockchain to container shipping. *Forbes.* Retrieved from https://www.forbes.com/sites/tomgroenfeldt/2017/03/05/ibm-and-maersk-apply-blockchain-to-container-shipping/.

Haughwot, J. (2015). Sensor Tech and IoT: Building the intelligent supply chain. *Manufacturing Business Technology.* Retrieved from http://www.mbtmag.com/article/2015/02/sensor-tech-and-iot-building-intelligent-supply-chain.

IBM. (2018). *IBM blockchain.* Retrieved from https://www.ibm.com/blockchain/industries/supply-chain.

Intel. (2018). *Intel.* Retrieved from Intel: https://www.intel.com/content/www/us/en/logistics-and-supply-chain/connected-logistics-platform/supply-chain-rogue-article.html?wapkw = supply + chain.

Kadiyala, A. (2018). Top emerging trends in 2018 for the supply chain. *Manufacturing Business Technology.* Retrieved from https://www.mbtmag.com/blog/2018/02/top-emerging-trends-2018-supply-chain.

Kim, M., & Chai, S. (2017). The impact of supplier innovativeness, information sharing and strategic sourcing on improving supply chain agility: Global supply chain perspective. *International Journal of Production Economics, 187*, 42–52. Available from https://doi.org/10.1016/j.ijpe.2017.02.007.

Krauth, O. (2018, February 9). 5 Companies using blockchain to drive their supply chain. *TechRepublic.* Retrieved from https://www.techrepublic.com/article/5-companies-using-blockchain-to-drive-their-supply-chain/.

Kshetri, N. (2018). 1 Blockchain's roles in meeting key supply chain management objectives. *International Journal of Information Management, 39*, 80–89. Available from https://doi.org/10.1016/j.ijinfomgt.2017.12.005.

Laaper, S., Yauch, G., Wellener, P., & Robinson, R. (2018, March 21). Embracing a digital future: How manufacturers can unlock the transformative benefits of digital supply networks. *Deloitte Insights.* Retrieved from https://www2.deloitte.com/insights/us/en/focus/industry-4-0/digital-supply-network-transformation-study.html.

Lanng, C. (2015, September 15). 5 Technological shifts that will change supply chains. *WeForum.* Retrieved from https://www.weforum.org/agenda/2015/09/5-technological-shifts-that-will-change-supply-chains/.

Lechmacher, W. (2016, August 4). As trade slows, what's next for global supply chains? *WeForum.* Retrieved from https://www.weforum.org/agenda/2016/08/as-trade-slows-whats-next-for-global-supply-chains.

Lehmacher, W., Betti, F., Beecher, P., Grotemeier, C., & Lorenzen, M. (2017, November 7). Impact of the fourth industrial revolution on supply chains. *WEF.* Retrieved from https://www.weforum.org/whitepapers/impact-of-the-fourth-industrial-revolution-on-supply-chains.

Liotine, M., Pagano, A. M., & Varma, S. (2016). *Technology trends in logistics and supply chain management.* Chicago, IL: Center for Supply Chain Management and Logistics, University of Illinois.

Manuj, I., & Mentzer, J. (2011). Global supply chain risk management. *Journal of Business Logistics*, *29*(1), 133–155. Available from https://doi.org/10.1002/j.2158-1592.2008.tb00072.x.

Margo, T. (2017, June 19). *Supply chain*. Retrieved from IBM: https://www.ibm.com/blogs/watson-customer-engagement/2017/06/19/blockchains-impact-b2b-networks/.

Mariani, J., Quasney, E., & Raynor, M. (2015, July 27). Forging links into loops: The Internet of Things' potential to recast supply chain management. *Deloitte Insights*. Retrieved from https://www2.deloitte.com/insights/us/en/deloitte-review/issue-17/internet-of-things-supply-chain-management.html.

Marr, B. (2017, August 29). How Walmart is using machine learning AI, IoT and big data to boost retail performance. *Forebes*. Retrieved from https://www.forbes.com/sites/bernardmarr/2017/08/29/how-walmart-is-using-machine-learning-ai-iot-and-big-data-to-boost-retail-performance.

MHI, & Deloitte. (2018). *The 2018 MHI annual industry report—overcoming barriers to NextGen supply chain innovation*. Retrieved from https://www.mhi.org/publications/report.

Microsoft. (2018). *Microsoft Azura*. Retrieved from https://azure.microsoft.com/en-us/solutions/?v = 18.28.

Milnes, H. (2017, June 16). How L'Oreal uses virtual reality to make internal decisions at its New York HQ. *Digitay*. Retrieved from https://digiday.com/marketing/loreal-uses-virtual-reality-make-internal-decisions-new-york-hq/.

Min, H. (2010). Artificial intelligence in supply chain management: Theory and applications. *International Journal of Logistics*, *13*(1), 13–39. Available from https://doi.org/10.1080/13675560902736537.

Min, H. (2016). Emerging trends of supply chain management: Where are we going? *Korean Journal of Logistics*, *24*(1), 1–9. Available from https://doi.org/10.15735/kls.2016.24.1.001.

Morales, J. (2015). Retrieved from stantonchase.com: http://www.stantonchase.com/wp-content/uploads/2015/07/Logistics-transportation-executives-facing-today-challenges-seek-solutions-well-into-the-future.pdf.

Morningstar. (2016). *Investing in the future: How to capitalize on exponential technologies ahead of the curve*. Morningstar Exponential Technologies Moat Focus Index.

Myerson, P. (2016, August 2). Supply chain technology brings the world closer together. *Industry Week*. Retrieved from http://www.industryweek.com/supply-chain/supply-chain-technology-brings-world-closer-together.

Myersen, P. (2018, February 9). It's not your dad's supply chain anymore. *Industrial Week*. Retrieved from https://www.industryweek.com/supply-chain-technology/it-s-not-your-dad-s-supply-chain-anymore.

Newman, D. (2018, January 9). How IoT will impact the supply chain. *Forbes*. Retrieved from https://www.forbes.com/sites/danielnewman/2018/01/09/how-iot-will-impact-the-supply-chain.

O'Byrne, R. (2018, January 2). How AI helps build the supply chain that thinks for itself. *Logistics Bureau*. Retrieved from https://www.logisticsbureau.com/how-ai-helps-build-the-supply-chain-that-thinks-for-itself/.

O'Marah, K. (2017, March 9). Blockchain for supply chain: Enormous potential down the road. *Forbes Magazine*. Retrieved from https://www.forbes.com/sites/kevinomarah/2017/03/09/blockchain-for-supply-chain-enormous-potential-down-the-road.

Oracle. (2016). Retrieved from https://Oracle.com/assets/idg-connect-report-infographic-3101243.pdf.

Oracle. (2018). Retrieved from https://cloud.oracle.com/en_US/supply-chain-planning-cloud/features.

Popper, N., & Lohr, S. (2017, March 4). Blockchain: A better way to track pork chops, bonds, bad peanut butter? *The New York Times*. Retrieved from https://www.nytimes.com/2017/03/04/business/dealbook/blockchain-ibm-bitcoin.htm.

Robinson, A. (2018, July 3). How supply chain systems integration is a game changer. *Industry Week*. Retrieved from https://www.industryweek.com/supply-chain/how-supply-chain-systems-integration-game-changer.

Rosenberg, A. (2016). *Next-Gen*. New York: SAP.

SAP. (2018). *SAP*. Retrieved from https://www.sap.com/products/supply-chain-iot/scm.html.

Schulman, D., Hajibashi, M., & Narsalay, R. (2018, May 14). Is your supply chain in sleep mode? *Accenture Consulting*. Retrieved from https://www.accenture.com/us-en/insights/industry-x-0/supply-chain-research.

Sehgal, V. (2010, July 26). Cost of sales and supply chain competence. *Supply Chain Musings*. Retrieved from http://www.supplychainmusings.com/2010/07/cost-of-sales-and-supply-chain.html.

Slone, R., Dittmann, J. P., & Mentzer, J. T. (2010). *The new supply chain agenda: The 5 steps that drive real value*. Boston, MA: Harvard Business School Publishing Corporation.

Srai, J. S. (2018, January 11). The digital supply chain revolution: A mountain worth climbing? *Supply chain and transport*. Retrieved from https://www.weforum.org/agenda/2018/01/the-digital-supply-chain-revolution-a-mountain-worth-climbing/.

Vollmer, M. (2018, July 5). Artificial intelligence: What's now and next In IoT-driven supply chain innovation. *Silicon semiconductor*. Retrieved from https://siliconsemiconductor.net/article/104738/Artificial_Intelligence_What.

Wolfson, R. (2018, July 11). Understanding how IBM and others use blockchain technology to track global food supply chain. *Forbes*. Retrieved from https://www.forbes.com/sites/rachelwolfson/2018/07/11/understanding-how-ibm-and-others-use-blockchain-technology-to-track-global-food-supply-chain/.

Yiannas, F. (2017, March 27). A new era of food transparency with Wal-Mart center in China. Retrieved from http://www.foodsafetynews.com/2017/03/a-new-era-of-food-transparency-with-wal-mart-center-in-china/.

Further reading

Barkai, J. (n.d.). What's the role of blockchain technology in the industrial Internet of Things? *Icons of infrastructure*. Retrieved from https://iconsofinfrastructure.com/the-internet-of-things-and-blockchain-when-overhyped-technologies-inte.

Blanchard, D. (2018, July 25). Top 25 supply chains of 2018. *Industry Week*. Retrieved from https://www.industryweek.com/supply-chain/top-25-supply-chains-2018.

Dignan, L. (2018, February 14). Top cloud providers 2018: How AWS, Microsoft, Google Cloud Platform, IBM Cloud, Oracle, Alibaba stack up. *ZDNet*. Retrieved from https://www.zdnet.com/article/cloud-providers-ranking-2018-how-aws-microsoft-google-cloud-platform-ibm-cloud-oracle-alibaba-stack/.

Evans, B. (2017, November 7). The top 5 cloud-computing vendors: #1 Microsoft, #2 Amazon, #3 IBM, #4 Salesforce, #5 SAP. *Forbes*. Retrieved from https://www.forbes.com/sites/bobevans1/2017/11/07/the-top-5-cloud-computing-vendors-1-microsoft-2-amazon-3-ibm-4-salesforce-5-sap/.

Google. (2018). Google cloud. Retrieved from Google: https://cloud.google.com/.

ITA, W. S. (2018, June 27). ICT as a development tool: Benefits, challenges & opportunities—The Philippine experience. Retrieved from https://www.wto.org/english/tratop_e/inftec_e/ita20th_e/08_lachica.pdf.

Lyall, A., Mercier, P., & Gstettner, S. (2018). *The death of supply chain management.*
Marr, B. (2018). Retrieved from https://www.bernardmarr.com/default.asp?contentID = 1354.
Mearian, L. (2018, June 1). Amazon joins list of blockchain-as-a-service providers. *Computerworld.* Retrieved from https://www.computerworld.com/article/3278088/blockchain/amazon-joins-list-of-blockchain-as-a-service-providers.html.
Srai, J., Christodoulou, P., Settanni, E., Harrington, T., Greitemann, J., Kumar, M., Beecher, P. (2017). *Next generation supply chains: Making the right decisions about digitalisation.* Retrieved from https://www.ifm.eng.cam.ac.uk/uploads/Resources/Reports/21.9.2017_IFM_GTR_DIGITAL_SUPPLY_CHAINS_AA_FINAL_WEB.pdf.

CHAPTER 4

The supply blockchain: integrating blockchain technology within supply chain operations

Matthew Liotine[1] and Don Ginocchio[2]
[1]Department of Information & Decision Sciences, University of Illinois at Chicago, Chicago, IL, United States
[2]SAP University Alliances, University of Notre Dame, Notre Dame, IN, United States

Contents

Technology in Supply Chain Management and Logistics
DOI: https://doi.org/10.1016/B978-0-12-815956-9.00004-1

Introduction

Blockchain is a technology concept with general purpose across many vertical industries, providing benefits by building upon existing business and operational models. Blockchain provides a social source of truth versus a single source of truth through a shared decentralized database model instead of a single centralized database system. It is a trust protocol built on elements of networking and cryptology that can be used to ensure trust without necessarily using an intermediary or central authority. In this respect, it can be used to create a reliable distributed digital ledger of record describing who owns what and who transacts with what. It is predicated on the simple idea that if everyone witnesses, believes, and agrees to something, then it is authentic and irrefutable. These features could generate enormous opportunities for innovating supply chain operations. This chapter will describe some fundamental characteristics of blockchain. It will then illustrate applications of its capabilities in the context of a smart contract. Potential use cases for application in various aspects of supply chain operations are discussed, representing those areas that are viewed as most fertile for first application. Finally, operational benefits and implementation caveats are summarized.

How it works

Blockchain was first introduced in a seminal work (Nakamoto, 2008). Blockchains are implemented on a distributed network of computers, called nodes, with each node representing a participant in the blockchain. The size of the network is indicative of trust among the parties. Blockchain is essentially a bookkeeping method that chains together ledger entries so that they are very difficult to modify later. This enables groups of unrelated parties to jointly keep a secure and reliable ledger of transactions recording a transfer of ownership of information between two parties. Instead of a central system, a shared protocol is utilized employing consensus algorithms so that all nodes agree upon what data comprises the legitimate blockchain.

Fig. 4.1 shows the transformation of a traditional supply chain network into a blockchain network. In the traditional hierarchical supply chain network, the movement of data through the network often mimics the flow of goods. In a distributed ledger environment using blockchain, all data and information can be shared in a decentralized fashion, with all parties seeing the same data. This eliminates the need for each supply chain partner acting as an intermediary between adjacent partners in sharing information. In the strictest sense, every node must be able to view transactions to be able to approve or reject them, but this depends on the nature of the supply chain application.

Each new transaction takes all the information from the previous transaction, including a unique key, and creates a new key, or cryptographic hash, which in essence is a digital fingerprint that is irreversible. Update or deletes (read/write) of a transaction are denied and are locked using private keys. Transactions are collected in blocks and organized in a tree structure known as a Merkle tree, as illustrated in Fig. 4.2. Prior to adding a transaction to a block, the identity of the party publishing the transaction is validated by other parties on the network and may also require the event or transaction itself to be validated by the others. The rules governing the consensus process can vary with the type of blockchain implementation.

Cryptographic keys are essential in ensuring privacy and the integrity of the blockchain. In Bitcoin, for example, every participant owns a pair of cryptographic keys—a public key, which is a publicly viewed identifier of the party, and a private key which is a secure identifier used to sign transactions (much like one's signature). The public key of a transaction's recipient is hashed with the originator's previous transaction and then signed with the originator's private key. This information is then hashed and used as the hashed transaction for the recipient's next transaction.

Blocks are validated before they are added to the blockchain to ensure that the information has not been tampered with. A calculation is then performed on each block's cryptographic hash, which can only be created from the exact data in the block. Each block includes the hash value of the previous block, thus interlocking new information with older information. A gossip or flooding algorithm is employed to inform parties on the network about the impending addition of the block. Each receives a current version of the block and decides to accept or reject it using the

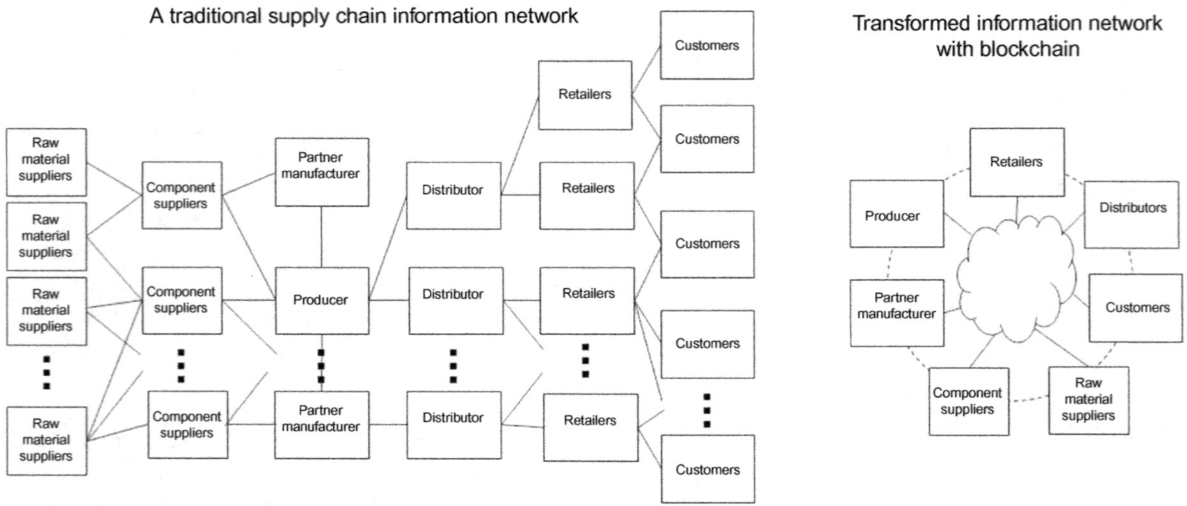

Figure 4.1 Transformation of a traditional supply chain information network with blockchain.

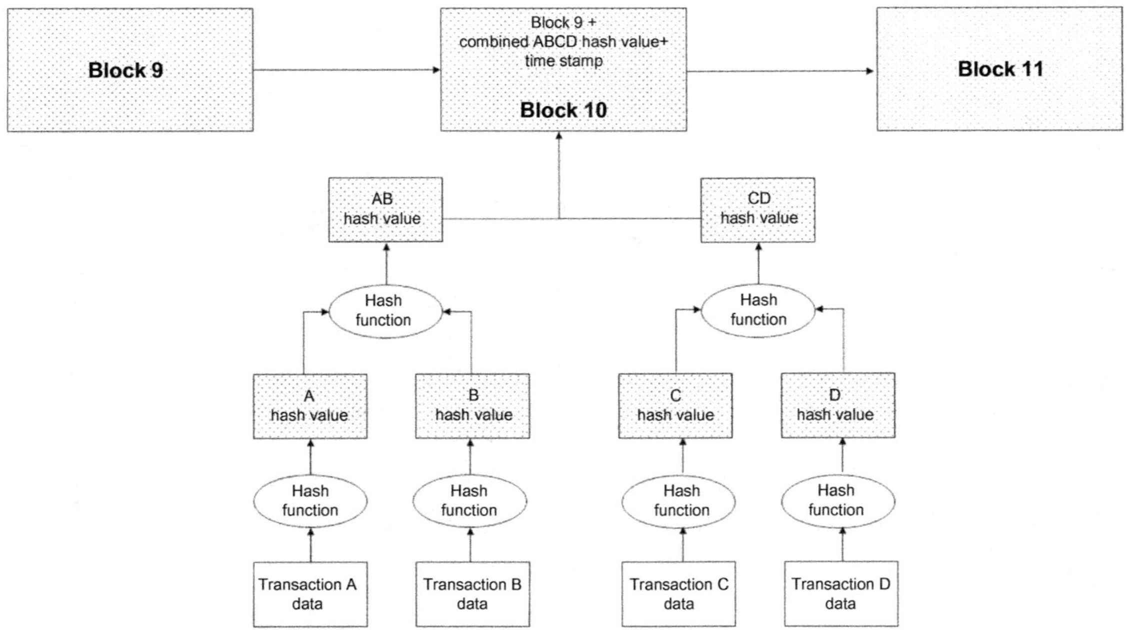

Figure 4.2 Merkle tree structure.

algorithm. In some blockchain standards, only certain parties on the network—referred to as "miners"—are charged with validating transactions and adding blocks.

The size of a block is indicative of consensus validation. Blocks are collected and stored as a chronological chain using a linked list of the hash pointers. Thus any change to either the original transaction data or the removal of transactions or blocks within a chain will result in a hash value differing from the one stored in the next block. Thus the blockchain is a true virtual ledger of the history of ownership of the piece of information, and any tampering of that data would be detected. All nodes will have the same view of transacted information represented by the hash value. If a node does not reflect the exact hash value as all other nodes, that node's data is not included in the blockchain. Thus there can be multiple copies of the blockchain until a consensus is achieved among nodes as to the legitimate copy.

Implementing blockchain requires special application software to establish governance of the blockchain. This includes enabling organizations to select the desired open blockchain standard, establish and trigger transactions, choose the appropriate communication protocols, size the peer network, select the cryptographic methods, and define the flooding and consensus algorithms, among other things. To minimize up-front capital investments and provide an easy low-risk adoption of blockchain technology, cloud-based blockchain as a service (BaaS) offerings are appearing.

Fully private or permissioned blockchains are used in situations where all participants on a blockchain already have a some degree of trust among them. They are more efficient since they involve less reliance on miners and assume that all network nodes are trusted, thereby reducing verification costs. The identity of those nodes adding blocks is known and assigned by the organization. This also has the advantage of more compatibility with preexisting privacy and compliance requirements.

Comparison of blockchain platforms

As of this writing, there are over 20 alternative blockchains, distributed ledgers, and/or blockchain related software products being developed and marketed. Table 4.1 (Valenta & Sandner, 2017) compares three that have shown promise for supply chain applications due to their ability to implement smart contracts (a topic that is discussed further in this chapter).

Table 4.1 Comparison of three major blockchain platforms.

	Blockchain platform		
Characteristic	**Ethereum**	**Hyperledger**	**R3 cords**
Description of platform	Generic blockchain platform	Modular blockchain platform	Specialized distributed ledger platform for financial industry
Governance	Ethereum developers	Linux Foundation	R3
Mode of operation	Permissionless, public or private	Permissioned, private	Permissioned, private
Consensus	• Mining based on proof-of-work (PoW) • Ledger level	• Broad understanding of consensus that allows multiple approaches • Transaction level	• Specific understanding of consensus(i.e., notary nodes) • Transaction level
Smart contracts	Smart contract code (e.g., Soliday)	Smart contract code (e.g., Go, Java)	• Smart contract code (e.g., Kotlin, Java) • Smart legal contract(legal prose)
Currency	• Ether • Tokens via smart contract	• Currency and tokens via chain code	None

Blockchain benefits

Blockchain is an enabler for maintaining symmetric information across a network. It can provide an alternative to realizing a consistent view of the same information distributed across many nodes using the principle of "once and done." Simply put, once a transaction is completed, it cannot be repudiated. Embedded within the hash value is transaction history information that cannot be easily altered or compromised, thereby making the information immutable. This proof of provenance renders the information as trustworthy when viewed by different participants at different nodes. The distributed nature of blockchains is somewhat counter to the concept of large, centralized databases.

This feature also eliminates the need for an intermediary system to house a centralized image of a piece of information, leading to cost savings in transaction verification and auditing (a concept known as costless verification). It also discourages transaction validation costs from outpacing transaction benefits, which is characteristic of information asymmetry (Catalini & Gans, 2016). It remains to be seen how the benefits of blockchain's ability to cost-effectively disintermediate information can outweigh the benefits of intermediation, such as curation and certification, as the network scales.

Use cases in vertical markets

Fundamental to blockchain is its ability to solve issues of trust. These include digitally validating a transaction that has occurred between two entities and rendering it irrefutable. When one considers the numerous kinds and volume of business transactions that occur daily, this fundamental capability can have profound impacts. Transactions such as land titles, loans, sales, intellectual property, procurement, identities, quality certification, votes, contract fulfillment, document verification, and so on lend themselves to this kind of capability. The following sections briefly describe some of the foremost applications of blockchain that are in use or that are currently being considered.

Banking and finance

Blockchain found its first home in the financial industry, where trust, security, and assurance are necessary to ensure the integrity of each monetary transaction. Digital currency is a virtual currency that is a monetary instrument associated with some artifact having value, and thus can be used as tender for payment of goods or services, or exchanged with other currencies, much like physical currency. While this concept is not entirely new, such implementation required the use of a central authority to manage the authenticity and security of transactions.

Blockchain enables the decentralized use of digital currency without the need for a central authority to spend time, money, and resources on verification. This enables the use of digital (and physical) currency in a low-cost way. It's built-in cryptography intrinsically enforces the integrity and prevents counterfeiting. The encryption also disjoins transactions from the identity of their participants. Bitcoin and Litecoin are examples of two premier digital currencies, among several others, who had each launched initial coin offerings of cryptocurrencies.

The ability to exchange currency securely in a decentralized fashion can open the door to enormous strides in improving the speed and integrity of monetary transactions across the globe. Coupled with the ability to connect networks through the Internet and increased service access through cloud computing, blockchain could enable the increase and inclusion of new markets for services such as digital currency, mobile payments, cross-border money transfers, and crowdfunding in a faster and secure manner.

Legal and intellectual property

Blockchain has also found a home in legal applications. Its ability to electronically provide reliable, authentic documentation of a transactions can lend itself for use in numerous legal use cases, replacing the need of vast amounts of paperwork, which is typically characteristic of legal transactions. One such example is the use of smart contracts, a concept which is fast becoming popular in many industries and which can drastically reduce transaction costs and embed specific contract conditions electronically within systems. Actions that are triggered automatically based on specific conditions through a smart contract can be automatically authenticated and secured. For example, a driver who is behind on his/her car payments may not be able to start his/her car. (Smart contracts are discussed in greater detail further in this chapter). In another example, some firms are using blockchain-based digital certificates to create an electronic paper trail for inventions and intellectual property that can automate and streamline dispute resolution.

Energy

Electrical energy in the form of electrons generated from the sun, wind, or other renewable sources is indistinguishable from that generated from fossil fuels. Keeping track of energy sources is an arduous and complex task, with many governments using a system of tradeable certificates. These systems require a registry that logs the generation of each unit of energy and creates certificates that are traded between buyers and sellers through a set of intermediaries. Instead, a blockchain-based platform could allow producers to trade energy between producers as well as with consumers. With a blockchain-based system, producers can get paid immediately (Orcutt, 2017). In this respect, blockchain can be used as an embedded mechanism to support self-generated power concepts, such as those currently being explored in Europe and developing nations. Here, it is being used to verify the amount of self-produced energy a user has contributed to the grid so that they can be billed or paid accurately.

Sustainability

Blockchain can be used as a way to legitimize and encode information obtained from farmers about their produce, including production quality and price. If placed in a distributed ledger, this information could be made available to second and third tier suppliers, making the supply and its associated sustainability information traceable and transparent. Financial lending institutions can then offer favorable credit based on evidence of sustainability. The availability of less expensive working capital would enable smaller businesses to increase investments in their farms to improve productivity without requiring additional land.

Healthcare

Blockchain can play a role in the digitalization of the healthcare industry. Health data interoperability follows three basic models: push, pull, and view. *Push* involves the sending of information from one provider to another. In the United States, a secure standard called Direct enables encrypted transmission between providers, requiring systems of provider directories and legal agreements for data sharing. *Pull* involves one provider querying information from another. *View* involves one provider viewing the data inside another provider's record.

These three operations are typically performed through informal ad hoc arrangements between organizations with no standardized audit trail and are subject to institutional policies, local medical practices, state laws, and national privacy enforcement. Blockchain opens up the possibility of establishing distributed ledgers with signatures that legitimize the medical records, making it cost-effective to securely share among providers, insurance companies, and patients. Such records could also be shared with researchers in a secure and controlled fashion to support medical studies (Halamka, Lippman, & Ekblaw, 2017).

Blockchain could also reduce the costs of tracking and tracing pharmaceuticals by serial number, batch, and expiration date, and can reduce the costs to verify drug and medical device authentication. The World Health Organization estimates that more than 8 percent of medical devices in circulation are counterfeit (Galer, 2017). The 2013 Drug Supply Chain Security Act (DSCSA) requires manufacturers of pharmaceutical products to serialize products at the lowest saleable level. Furthermore, supply chain participants must share certain production, trading partner, and ownership information of the product. This requires supply chain participants to use electronic systems to trace products from the manufacturer, which implies the intermediation of volumes of information between previously unknown entities—a genuinely daunting task. However, blockchain's ability to disintermediate information could create instant trust more cost-effectively than a single centralized system.

Media, arts, and entertainment

In the media, arts, and entertainment sectors, blockchain again has the potential to eliminate or dramatically lower transaction costs. For example, blockchain could enable a news website to charge readers per article, rather than per month, without paying fees to a payment platform. A blockchain ledger could be used to protect intellectual property, like music and film, by providing verification of authenticity for content, thereby enforcing usage rights and discouraging piracy during content distribution.

Advertising

Blockchain can create an opportunity for consumers to control and monetize their personal identifying information. Blockchain can be used to reveal only those portions of a personal identity that can be shared with an advertiser or consumer surveyor, and how much they would be required to pay for it.

Smart contracts

At the heart of a blockchain's appeal for use in the supply chain is the smart contract, which in essence is a self-executing contract. It is a set of logic based on rules that govern business transactions that are embodied within computer software and distributed across a blockchain network whose nodes represent supply chain participants. When executed, the logic determines if and how a transaction is posted to the blockchain. For example, smart contract logic might check to see if an invoice from a registered agent has been reconciled with purchase orders (PO) and then send payment to a supplier when a shipment is received, signaled via the blockchain fabric.

Smart contracts require tremendous coordination and agreement and clarity on conditions and actions as to how they will be verified and enforced. The following are some of the components involved in creating a smart contract:

- *Contract composition*—A contract originator must create a contract, which can be customized for different purposes. Software code, called chain code, must be written that embodies the rules of the contract. The contract would be created in a form similar to an extended finite state machine.
- *Network definition*—Users must define the network of parties that will be incorporated within the smart contract execution.
- *Deployment*—The contract must be deployed on a selected blockchain fabric. Before deployment, users can test the contract for any flaws or functionality using a simulated environment. Fig. 4.3 illustrates the contract creation and deployment architecture.
- *Agents*—Once a contract is created and deployed, distributed applications, called software agents, dispersed across the network must interact with the blockchain fabric on behalf of a party. Agents can be activated on a platform of choice, such as a computer or networked appliance, or reside on a cloud, based on the type of use of the contract. Agents view the blockchain and will update it based on events and conditions that they continuously monitor per those defined by the smart contract. Exception and error handling situations must be addressed within the creation of the contract code.
- *Monitoring*—Once deployed, the contract originator can monitor the status of the contract via a dashboard with standard or user-defined key performance indicators (KPIs). Agents report status to the contract

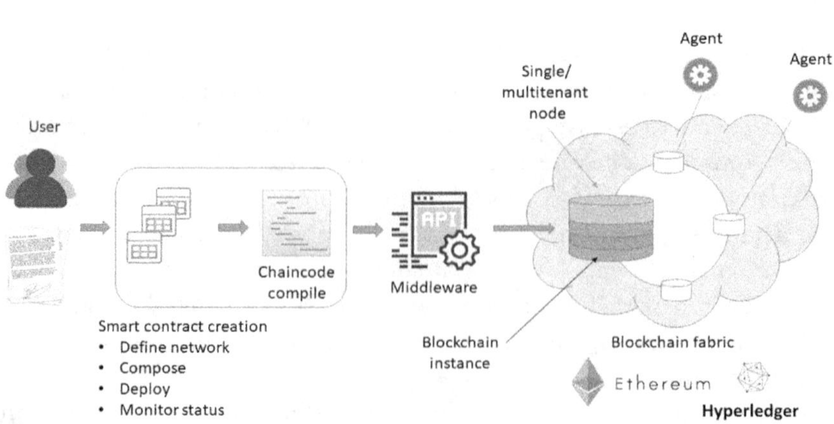

Figure 4.3 Smart contract creation and deployment.

originator—as well as all other parties—based on the information contained within the blockchain.

The following simple example entails the creation of a PO for raw materials from a supplier. The transactions are modeled after those found in a typical ERP system. The process is as follows:

1. The buying firm issues a PO to a supplier for a quantity of material to be delivered by a particular date.
2. The supplier sends the material to the buyer.
3. The buyer performs a quality inspection of the material.
4. If the material passes inspection, the buyer creates a goods receipt.
5. If the material passes inspection, the buyer pays the invoice when it is received from the buyer.
6. If the material does not pass inspection, the material is returned to the supplier.
7. If the material does not pass inspection, the buyer does not pay the invoice when it is received from the buyer.

There could be other stipulations in the buyer-supplier agreement that are not represented in the above for the sake of simplicity. For example, if the delivery is late, there could be a monetary penalty that is invoked, or if the material does not pass inspection, the supplier may still accept it but it is downgraded to lower quality and thus a price reduction is paid when the invoice is received.

The ledger

The smart contract process begins by determining what items get recorded in the distributed ledger. The ledger would serve as an audit trail for the material. A key question is what variables are needed to characterize the transactions, how is the asset to be digitized, and what variables are required by both parties to assure proof of provenance. This has to be agreed up-front by all parties, and variables that are agreed upon are then included in the ledger. The ledger would resemble that shown in Table 4.2.

Some issues would need to be rectified. First, the fields to serve as keys for information retrieval need to be identified. Furthermore, while digital keys are encrypted, they may not necessarily be reencrypted per transaction if desired, depending on the type of network and blockchain fabric that is used. For brevity, 12-character keys and hash values are shown. The Transaction Type and Pass Inspection field values can be

Table 4.2 Distributed ledger example.

Transaction	Transaction type	Origin ID	Destination ID	Asset	PO date	Deliver date	Amount	Quantity	Pass inspection	Invoice	Chain
TRANSID	TTYPE	ORID	DESTID	MID	PODATE	DDATE	AMT	QTY	PINSP	INVID	
1	PO	ed7hs/gdr2z4	krofg28sqav8	10097	12/15/2017	1/8/2018	$15,000	100			ocDgFeI1278k
2	Quality Inspection	ed7hs/gdr2z5	krofg28sqav8	10097	12/15/2017	1/8/2018	$15,000	100	Yes		bcgRg89bdfg8
3	Goods Receipt	ed7hs/gdr2z6	krofg28sqav8	10097	12/15/2017	1/8/2018	$15,000	100	Yes		8hsp9cHGkn4P
4	Invoice	ed7hs/gdr2z7	krofg28sqav8	10097	12/15/2017	1/8/2018	$15,000	100	Yes	27915	Owyyc8msLRSc

codified, which is more typical in ERP systems but is not done in this example for illustrative purposes. Note that many more variables can be included in the ledger—we limited the example to a few, just for illustrative purposes. Both parties have a copy of the ledger and can view it at any time, and thus have an audit trail for the material.

If one of the parties breaches the ledger and tries to alter the chained information, this would prevent the next transaction from being chained or added to a block due to a nonconsensus situation (exception handling for this scenario needs to be defined). Furthermore, if one of the parties breaches the ledger and tries to alter the nonchained information, then the system must determine how to handle this exception. For example, perhaps the chain is recomputed when this occurs, and it is determined that is has been altered, leading to another nonconsensus situation. The chain fabric in use would have to be examined to determine how such exceptions are handled.

Creating the smart contract

The smart contract would be created using the following steps:

1. Identify the network of peers.
2. Identify the asset(s) that are being exchanged.
3. Define the list of transaction types.
4. For each transaction type, identify the list of triggers and the resulting conditional events.
5. Determine what gets recorded in the ledger.
6. Define what information gets chained.

In our example, there are two peers: the buyer and the supplier. The asset is the material denoted by the MID with the associated quantity QTY that is being purchased. In this example, we obtain values from the ERP system to help drive the smart contract:

PID = the PO document number

QSPECT = quality inspection indicator

GR = goods receipt indicator

INVID = invoice document number

INPD = invoice paid indicator

Table 4.3 shows how the transaction types are defined for exchange among the peers. In this example, all items written to the ledger are chained, but not all items need to be chained. Both parties have a copy of the ledger.

Table 4.3 Definition of transaction types.

Ttype	Triggers	Events	Variable	Ledgered	Chained
PO	PID≠0	Set PO confirmation	POISS	Y	Y
		Set the PO date	PODATE	Y	Y
		Set the transaction ID	TRID	Y	Y
		Set the material	MID	Y	Y
		Set the quantity	QTY	Y	Y
Quality Inspection	QSPECT = Y	Pass quality inspection	QSPECT	Y	Y
Goods Receipt	GR = Y	Goods receipt posted	GR	Y	Y
Invoice Paid	INPD = Y	Invoice paid	INPD	Y	Y
			INVID	Y	Y

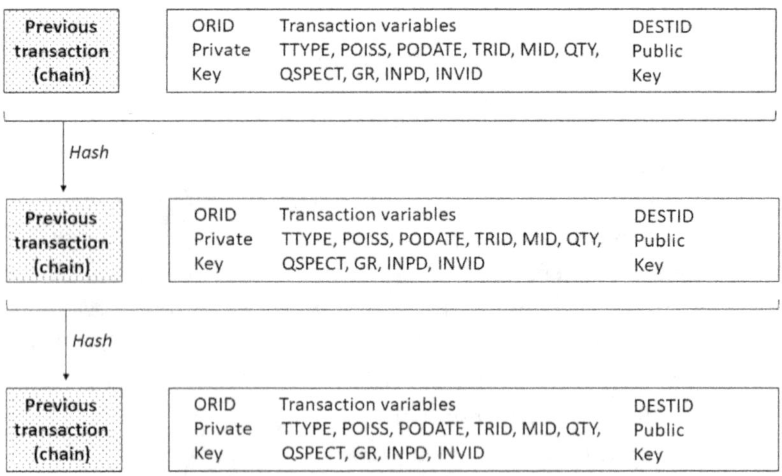

Figure 4.4 Forming a blockchain of transactions.

The blockchain process

The blockchain is written as part of the ledger, as illustrated in Fig. 4.4, along with other variables and data that can be viewable. Additional information can be added as agreed upon by the parties.

Supply chain use cases

Blockchain's potential extends far beyond cryptocurrency applications and is already viewed as an underlying mechanism that can improve supply chain efficiency and efficacy. The global supply chain is worth over $40 trillion annually. Logistics requires complex international regulations that govern the movement of goods around the globe, tying up inventory and creating the overhead costs of managing the movement. The information involved is voluminous and is prone to error or corruption among the intermediaries involved, due to the presence of information asymmetries.

The ability to bestow instant trust within recorded transactions can lend itself to improving efficiencies within the many functions that are characteristic of supply chain operations, including monetary exchanges, operational transactions, contracting, and sourcing, among others, without the exclusive need of a centralized system. The fact that it serves as a distributed ledger enables end-to-end documentation to track and trace where and how materials are sourced, purchased, allocated, and used. Transparency and accountability can thus be improved, and materials can be more easily authenticated with regard to their source and quality. This can accelerate the flow of goods, help control product recalls, and provide additional transparency into logistics activities. More vertical integration would be encouraged since the costs associated with moving products among intermediaries would be reduced with improved transparency (Pan, 2016).

The following are examples of use cases that demonstrate blockchain's potential in reducing supply chain costs and improving service levels.

Sourcing

Sourcing is viewed as a prime area of application for blockchain. Purchasing organizations can evaluate supplier value and risk in real time based on detailed information about how their materials are sourced, manufactured, and shipped. Since transactions between a vendor and its partners can be made visible to others in the chain, purchasing organizations can gage a supplier's performance and obtain the knowledge to negotiate better prices. Such information can also provide visibility of cost distribution across the supply chain. Economically providing visibility would reduce the friction costs of creating more complex supply networks, and would open the door for smaller suppliers to participate in the supply chain's value network. Furthermore, suppliers might be able to submit quotes directly to the supply chain, such that the order is affixed to the distributed ledger and suppliers need onboarded to the blockchain only once. Additionally, the information can be shared with insurers to negotiate transportation coverage with logistics providers and producers.

Track and trace

Information asymmetry and inconsistency is ever present among supply chain participants, creating obstacles to tracking specific transactions and goods. Downstream participants will often require information regarding a product, including its assembly process, material lists, and precautionary warnings. Quite often, the integrity of a product's transaction history requires extensive processes and controls that are not easily achievable. Used in conjunction with a distributed ledger, the transfer of goods between two parties, identified as two addresses in the blockchain, can be recorded. The transaction would include additional information such as location, date, price, and quantity. The blockchain can render each transaction record as irrefutable, enabling all parties who access the ledger the ability to trace ingredients or components to their legitimate place of origin (Lohr & Popper, 2017).

Serialization is the assignment of unique traceable numbers to individual items. Products need to be serialized in order to track and trace them (following the product) and conducting verification at certain points as they move through the supply chain to ensure its legitimacy. Many countries require that such information is reported to a responsible government agency and/or other supply chain partners. This information is often required to be retained for about 12 years. The GS1 standard, established by the Internet Corporation for Assigned Names and Numbers (ICANN), is used by much of the world to establish a standardized method of serialization. It employs a two-dimensional (2D) barcode that contains a variety of information, including the company's Global Trade Identification Number (GTIN), a product identifier, expiration date, and additional data (Tracelink, 2015). Work is underway to associate barcodes with blockchain hash values, such that a product's transaction history can be easily traced. In the pharmaceutical industry, standards work is underway to address this need relative to compliance with federal regulations. This is discussed later in this chapter.

Payment processing

Blockchain can also be used to improve supply chain payment processing, particularly in those situations where buyers use a supply chain finance

(SCF) platform to increase the net terms of payment to their suppliers. The buyer contracts with an SCF provider or bank, which also supports the suppliers. Suppliers submit invoices to the buyer through the SCF platform. The buyer then approves the invoice, triggering a payment to the supplier from the SCF platform. The supplier receives the payment, which is discounted in return for receiving the payment sooner and covers the SCF provider's service fees. The buyer will then pay the SCF provider the full amount due per negotiated payment terms. The amount of the discount is typically based on the buyer's credit rating such that a high-risk buyer would result in higher fees and discounts on payments. The SCF provider could sell the receivables to another party to reduce credit exposure, or hedge against the risk using credit default swaps.

A blockchain executed smart contract could be used to make this overall process more efficient by encoding and enacting the atomic transactions based on the state of a ledger, versus rules dictated through an SCF platform. The transaction information need not be necessarily centralized within a common SCF platform, reducing the costs of service fees. So, for example, payment for invoices can be authenticated and made immediately to the supplier upon recognition.

Logistics and shipping

The ability to track the shipment of a container from origin to destination with every transaction along the way has historically been a major supply chain challenge and has not changed much in the last 50 years. The process is complex and involves nearly 30 entities, including importers, exporters, freight forwarders, clearing agents, shipping lines, haulage companies, intermodal operators, surveyors, banks, tax officials, health organizations and insurance brokers. The process is manual and paper-based and involves hundreds of communication events that centers upon the chain of custody for just one container. It requires about 55 documents, including commercial invoices, packing lists, certificates of origin, shipping instructions, bills of lading (the standard contract of carriage), cargo inspection certificates, customs clearance documents, freight invoices, and letters of credit that can be used to guarantee a transaction (Smith, 2018). Another layer of tracking is the ability to track the quantity, specification, and origin of containers, trailers, and pallets.

Blockchain can be used to simplify the shipping processes and greatly reduce the time to process a shipment by encoding the insurance quotes, customs clearances, and duty information directly to a shipment. A distributed digital ledger can be used to maintain transactions that are blockchained. Transactions and information such as packing lists, invoices, certificates of origins, export approvals, import licenses, delivery instructions and necessary clearances, bill of lading, marine insurance, and cargo inspection certificates, can be loaded into the ledger from the relevant parties. This can provide full visibility of a container's documents and procedural transactions to clearing agents, shipping lines, haulers, intermodal operators, and surveyors and reduce costs by eliminating paperwork, manual processing, duplication of effort, time delays and the times to process the shipment through its journey, including customs clearance time.

These benefits can unlock working capital that is tied up while product is in transit and reduce losses, particularly in the case of the spoilage of perishable goods. It can also ensure completeness and accuracy of documentation and reduce documentation tampering and fraud from the original PO through delivery to the consignee warehouse. This is because transactions recorded on a blockchain are immutable such that no party can fraudulently alter the records. The transparency afforded by a distributed ledger can be used effectively to allocate resources by posting other information, such as capacity, cost, and estimated delivery times for different routes used on different shipping lanes. Such information can be used to plan shipments and dynamically adjust pricing based on supply and demand. Overall, the use of blockchain to enhance global logistics transactions could improve free trade between companies and countries by reducing the costs of intermediaries such as freight brokers. These cost reductions can reduce costs for carriers and ultimately reduce consumer prices.

Supply integrity and safety

The issue of supply provenance has been ongoing within the food industry, with about 10% of people falling ill or dying from contaminated food each year. In addition, counterfeit or illegitimate food products cost consumers millions of dollars. However, the problem of provenance of supply is not only restricted to food but includes a wide variety of goods, including clothing, diamonds, automotive parts and supplies, and electronics, among others. The complexity of today's supply chains makes it difficult for retailers, producers, and consumers to verify the authenticity of a product's ingredients and components, and to uncover any wrong-doings with regard to ethical sourcing, child labor, counterfeiting, or other unethical methods that may have been used in creating the product.

In the food industry, producers are exploring ways to utilize blockchain to track food products made from poultry, beef, pork, and produce from the farm to processing lines and to the retail store. So, for example, the information about a shipment of a particular produce item arriving at a factory could be blockchained and stored in a distributed ledger, together with information about the product, factory, and other pertinent details, to remain available for verification when needed. Such details could include quality control data, temperature, shipment, delivery dates, safety certifications, and even the credentials of the employees carrying out specific tasks. These applications can also leverage sensor technology that can measure characteristics such as shock, temperature, and humidity, and record this information within the ledger. Depending on the nature or value of the product, such information could be used to detect potential product damage. Every input, conversion step, including sterilization and disinfection, and output along the way from supply to customer could be recorded and coded in the ledger.

This not only can improve product safety, but it can also reduce trace times from days to seconds, which can consequently lead to operational cost savings. Furthermore, the data stored in the ledger can be used for descriptive analytics to identify production bottlenecks, and support food safety audits more cost-effectively. Consumers may be able to trace the entire supply chain of a product by simply scanning the product's code.

While the food industry is a prime candidate for these use cases, similar ones can be devised for other kinds of products. For example, pharmaceuticals must also require similar precautions within their production and distribution processes. Nonconsumable goods, such as textiles and diamonds could also benefit. Blood diamonds and conflict minerals require proof or provenance for reasons of legitimacy in their movement from mines to consumers. This includes knowing where the item was sourced, possessions of ownership, authenticity, certifications, and safety characteristics.

Insurance

Blockchain's features can be combined with Internet of Things (IoT), sensors, and data analytics to characterize a shipment's journey and help predict delays, diversions, damages, and arrival times. A shared ledger that can log information about such risks can be used to help shippers better comply with insurance regulations. For example, if ledgers indicate geographical areas known for piracy, insurers can offer special coverages for ships heading for those regions. Insurance claims could potentially be paid sooner since blockchained information within the ledger can be used to quickly settle claims without having to pour through the voluminous documentation required to verify a claim.

Used in conjunction with smart contract capabilities, insurers can act in (near) real time to changes in the state of a product during its shipment. This includes tracing and validating when and where handovers occurred, authenticating ownership and the condition of an asset at each point in its chain of custody. This capability would be of particular importance for high-value assets, such as diamonds, fine art, and wine, which are often subject to fraudulent activity. Such ledger information would not only be of value to insurers, but also to other parties, such as owners, shippers, banks, and logistics providers who participate in a product's movement. Using blockchain within the ledger would ensure that the information is immutable since it cannot be changed or removed.

Smart pallets

Blockchain connected smart pallets could make it easier to locate and optimize pallet utilization. This could reduce costs associated with unused, lost, or stolen pallets, and lead to new or improved business models for such processes as vendor-managed inventory, automatic customs clearance, and pay per use. It can also improve production scalability and flexibility. For example, when a customer's pallet within a warehouse triggers a PO for more material to support a production line, it is immediately validated using blockchain protocols and quickly expedited to the supplier's network.

Trucking

Used in conjunction with self-executing smart contracts, blockchain technology could enable shippers to pay drivers automatically upon freight delivery or reimbursement upon refueling. It can be used to track vehicle ownership possession, ensuring driver record accuracy, automate vehicle maintenance records, and trace any tampering with sensitive cargo such as food (Staff, 2017). Maintenance crews can have confidence that software downloaded to a 3D printer to print a new part for a vehicle can be trusted. Altogether, such capabilities can provide the basis for new business models of logistics transport, such as trucking companies renting time for trailer usage within universal trailer pools. Information captured within vehicles identified as trusted endpoint systems can be sold to the network, creating new models for the delivery of goods.

Blockchain standards efforts

Blockchain will impact how policymakers approach regulation, safety, and monitoring since it enhances the ability to enforce design standards through a structured protocol. There exists a wide range of industry-specific and general directives regarding the confidentiality, integrity, and availability of data in the United States and in many other countries. These will likely require that blockchain solutions comply with their stipulations. For example, in the United States, blockchain solutions for sharing and recording patient records are subject to the US Health Insurance Portability and Accountability Act (HIPAA). In Europe, personal data is protected by the General Data Protection Regulation (GDPR), which includes requirements for the export of personal data outside the European Union.

Nevertheless, at the time of this writing, there is a lack of common vertical industry standards and only a few noteworthy efforts underway related to blockchain:

- *ISO/TC 307—Blockchain and Distributed Ledger Technologies*

  This effort is establishing terminology and underlying concepts dealing with privacy and personally identifiable information protection, security risks and vulnerabilities, identity, reference architectures, and a common taxonomy and ontology.
- *Blockchain in Transport Association (BiTA)*

  This is a technology trade group for the development of blockchain standards and education for the freight industry. The forum was formed by several leading freight technology and transportation companies to gather firms that could benefit from blockchain, including technology vendors, equipment manufacturers, suppliers, consultants, banks, carriers, shippers, logistics companies, and freight brokers.
- *Wall Street Blockchain Alliance (WSBA)*

  This is an alliance (not a standards body) comprised of financial institutions with interest in financial opportunities, to seek blockchain solutions to financial challenges in supply chain management applications. For these purposes, it has partnered with the BiTA group.

- *International Telecommunications Union (ITU-T)*

  This longtime European telecommunication standards body is focusing on security and privacy aspects of blockchain in telecommunications.

- *Drug Supply Chain Security Act (DSCSA)*

  The DSCSA was enacted by the U.S. Congress on November 27, 2013, to outline steps to build an interoperable system to identify and trace certain prescription drugs as they are distributed. The main purpose of the legislation is to protect consumers from drugs that may be counterfeit, stolen, contaminated, or harmful. The DSCSA requires wholesale distributors and third-party logistics providers to report licensure and tracing information annually to the Federal Drug Administration (FDA). The GS1 standards group, as previously mentioned, has issued a standard called the GS1 Electronic Product Code Information Services (EPCIS), for DSCSA lot-level management, serialization, and item-level traceability. This involves sharing data among manufacturers, wholesalers, repackagers, and pharmacies (both hospitals and retail) in the form of transaction information (TI), transaction history (TH), and transaction statements (TS) at the lot (or batch) level of identification. Item serialization requires manufacturer and repackagers to serialize packages of drug products using a product identifier, either a GS1 Global Trade Item Number (GTIN) or National Drug Code (NDC), and serial number (SGTIN), lot number (LGTIN), and expiration date. Serialized item-level traceability requires making available information that would allow supply chain partners to trace the ownership back to the original manufacturer or repackager.

The Center for Supply Chain Studies recently organized an ad hoc initiative involving many pharmaceutical industry players to develop a standard reference model to identify the extraction of information from EPCIS transactions involving a pharmaceutical to a shared blockchain for DSCSA compliance (Center for Supply Chain Studies, 2018). The issues with developing such a model centered around the determination of exactly what information should be blockchained (on-chain) versus kept off the chain (off-chain). Several issues became apparent:

- It was found that it was not feasible nor practical to store all serialized EPCIS transactions (e.g., commissioning, packing, shipping, receiving) between trading partners, due to the volumes of information that would have to be processed and stored.

- While the DSCSA requires sharing transaction information across trading partners, it is not necessary that all detailed transaction information has to be ledgered and accessed by everyone.
- Such information could be appended with such that can be used for operational purposes as well as by trading partners. It would be necessary to identify which information would satisfy the common needs of trading partners.
- The TI/TS information to be on-chained should be such that the exchange of the same information outside the blockchain would not be necessary.
- An additional identifier called the shipping container code (SSCC) could be useful in identifying logistic units (i.e., containers) for traceability.

Instead of on-chaining transactions, the resulting reference model was formulated and is illustrated in Fig. 4.5. It is based on the strategy of transforming and condensing transaction data off-chain into agreed upon transactional state tables that can be efficiently on-chained. States can be defined such as fit for commerce, in-commerce, provenance whether the item is DSCSA exempt. Transactions can be referenced, if needed, using pointers or addresses versus storing all the transaction's information within the blockchain down to the pallet, case, or package level. Thus the blockchain serves as an extension of localized transaction data to augment centralized data.

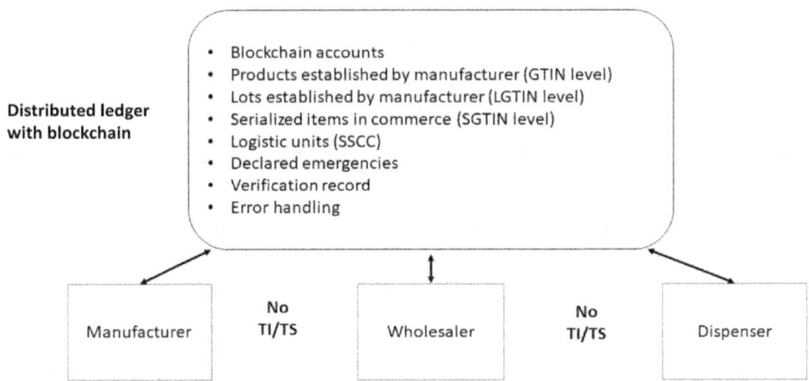

Figure 4.5 DSCSA proposed blockchain reference standard.

Enacting the reference model within the EPCIS framework also revealed some additional issues. These include error and exception processing (e.g., replacing an erroneous on-chain transaction with a new one); creating additional transactions for chaining (e.g., documenting the verification check of a drug); the handling of different GLN identifiers for the same transaction partner due to state law requirements; and the ability to verify nonadjacent transaction partners in the case of a saleable return. This last scenario involves how a manufacturer can verify whether a received return originated from an authorized nonadjacent downstream transaction partner. This would require an indication implicit within the product that it was originally placed into commerce by the manufacturer and is not counterfeit.

Blockchain caveats

The caveats of blockchain arise from the fact that it is faced with challenges that produce risks that are usually characteristic of emerging technologies. In addition, there are many misconceptions regarding blockchain that need to be reconciled to avoid major pitfalls across many levels. Foremost, relevant industry and government directives have yet to be fully defined, thereby increasing risks for organizations wanting to assimilate blockchain solutions within their operations. Furthermore, solutions must ensure that confidentiality, integrity, and availability follow data through its life cycle stages, such as collection, storage, utilization, transfer, and destruction. The following are some caveats that stem from these quandaries.

- *Intermediaries may still exist*

  Blockchain is simply a combination of protocols and technology to form a distributed consensus-driven database. While the database is created by validating transactions as they are created between parties without the use of a central authority or intermediary, other forms of intermediation may still exist, such as the software or cloud network used. Furthermore, it remains to be seen if disintermediation effectively reduces transaction cost, since this is quite often the argument for intermediation, as exemplified in computer networking.
- *Privacy is still required*

  The systems engineering process involved in developing a blockchain solution must embed privacy within the overall system design from beginning to end. Organizations must also see that right-sized privacy principles provide reasonable privacy of information transacted in the blockchain. Any exposure of blockchain transaction or user metadata could reveal private user information. Users transacting under multiple pseudonyms is a way to safeguard against this.

- *Access control and key protection is a major issue*

  Security weaknesses persist at endpoints accessing a blockchain application regarding securely storing cryptographic keys that are used as digital signatures. If a digital key is made public, some encrypted content could be accessible to hackers or invite unwanted peers. This mandates the design, implementation, and maintenance of endpoint security controls such as authentication and firewalls as well as network and system monitoring to identify incidents. Once they have given their personal data away, users will have limited control over their data due to the immutable nature of blockchain. Limiting key protection to a few parties may reduce the work of an attacker to a smaller number of targets that could be hacked.

- *Trust in system design*

  Developing a blockchain solution requires arduous modification of existing systems and processes. Blockchain services must operate visibly and transparently and assure users that the service is performing according to stated promises. Blockchain solution designs must align tightly with their functional requirements to trust that the code and network function and perform as expected. To this end, solutions must support audit and verification functions (Sathiyamurthy, 2017). This requirement not only pertains to the system itself but also to other systems that it interfaces with.

  In a "code is law" environment, incomplete rule sets may permit undesirable behavior. The concept of applying machine governance to social systems can have a disastrous impact on investment and business decisions if flaws exist in the software code. Code may be law for machines, but the law is code for the people (Murck, 2017). Consensus mechanisms within code can pose additional technical, ethical, and compliance challenges. Technically, the choice of consensus protocol can have a significant impact on performance and operational capacity. Some protocols provide incentives for strategically voting, preventing voting based on sincere preference.

- *Regulations and homogeneous of standards are necessary*

  Regulations, standards, and best practices should qualify most aspects of a blockchain solution to confirm the integrity, including that of the code, algorithms, platforms, and operational and performance standards. Since everything cannot practically be qualified, industry best practices should identify safeguards and checks necessary in development and operation. Furthermore, interoperability among blockchain protocols is limited, and there are no clear interoperability standards among the different blockchain protocols as of this writing.

Another dilemma facing blockchain implementation in supply chains is that network nodes residing in different jurisdictions can create legal and compliance issues regarding the legality and enforceability of records or code due to differences in laws across the jurisdictions. Since data could exist in a decentralized fashion across different regions and systems, reconciliation and synchronization across systems may be challenging (Caron, 2017). This problem is further compounded when information resides on systems using different blockchain fabrics since interoperability among different fabrics is very limited. Such challenges become visible when dealing with the myriad of historical international laws and regulations that govern freight logistics between different countries, which would likely require monumental revision.

- *Cryptography still requires safeguards*

  Since blockchain is founded on the strength of hashing and encryption algorithms that are used throughout, they must always be kept updated as hackers improve their proficiency. If used in a distributed ledger, safeguards should be employed to prevent hackers from altering the hash value. Even though the blockchain protocol can intrinsically know if this happens, hacking opportunities should be discouraged.

- *Node integrity should not be overlooked*

  The security and integrity of the platforms housing the very nodes that comprise the blockchain network require continuous attention. While these nodes are still susceptible to cyberattacks such as denial of service attacks, the possibility of dominant processors controlling the blockchain can exist if all systems, or at least those involved in consensus making, are operated by the same entity or by bad players. This also concentrates power in a handful of entities which could politicize the network.

- *Transaction curation and finality must be assured*

  While blockchain assures that everyone sees the same information across a network, the information can still be wrong. Thus the processes used to generate transactions must be standardized and automated to ensure trustworthy exchanges, and exception handling and systemic monitoring must be used to sense nonconformities and erroneous events. Since transactions are hashed, there is no direct way to confirm their integrity, except to say that they have not been altered. Deviations or errors in processing transactions involving shared persistent data could create joint liability and indemnity disputes. Such errors would be difficult to correct and might require a trusted third party authorized to correct them across multiple nodes.

Distributed consensus protocols are usually based on computational proof-of-work and provide only probabilistic finality. This means that a transaction is never truly final due to the possibility that a longer chain has been created that does not include the block of the transaction, but this becomes less computationally viable as blocks are added. Transaction finality can be an area of dispute, particularly in the financial industry, which has strict requirements for transaction finality.

- *Transaction volume*

  Recording every single transaction for a given product on a blockchain-based ledger may be prohibitive due to the number and volumes of product transactions. The sheer size of transaction information could overwhelm the processing capacity of those systems that support a blockchain. Furthermore, sensitive information within transactions may not necessarily want to be shared. Instead, alternative ways of providing data to the blockchain in avenues other than transaction data may be required. Analysis may be required to determine whether asset state information can be shared among trading partners or if sharing should be restricted to transaction data.

- *Private or public blockchains*

  Public or permissionless blockchains such as Bitcoin are open to anyone and everyone and allow users to participate in transactions and review codified rules. This feature alone makes them susceptible to many of the caveats mentioned above. Private or permissioned blockchains restrict access to preselected, trusted participants, thereby enabling more efficient consensus protocols and greater privacy. They permit more active management and governance of encoded rules and procedures to react to exceptions or disruptions. Participants will likely have different roles and responsibilities, like those found in supply chain networks, such as producer, supplier, retailer, or customer.

Prescription for blockchain

Blockchain can decrease transaction costs and create added transparency without the need for a centralized intermediary party or system. Used in conjunction with a distributed ledger, it provides a highly efficient way of synchronizing data across many parties such that they all see the same data. These features provide attractive opportunities for implementation within supply chain operations. While there are many pilots underway to explore these opportunities, it is common for many firms to take a "wait and see" approach before implementing blockchain related solutions within their own operations.

As with any new and innovative technology, a low-risk approach is usually desirable. To this end, the following are some guidelines for pursuing a successful blockchain initiative. Each of these guidelines provides criteria for realizing blockchain benefits:

- *Multipoint information exchange*

  Keeping information centralized across multiple participants in a supply chain should be weighed against the benefits of decentralization. Centralized databases are often used to support multipoint information exchange, versus point-to-point. If the operational and storage costs of centralizing data with shared write access are excessive, then this could present an opportunity for replacing the centralized database with a distributed ledger. A blockchain protocol could provide the mechanisms to receive and distribute information across a network and keep that information synchronized so that everyone sees the same thing, thus serving as an internal reflection of trust. In turn, this would eliminate the costs of using middlemen or intermediaries to provide a centralized data service.
- *Verification of transactions*

  Transaction integrity and security are extremely important within the supply chain. A trusted third-party intermediary is traditionally required based on the assumption that supply chain participants do not know or trust one another or may have misaligned interests. Hence, an intermediary's role is that of securing, curating, controlling, and validating transactions across multiple participants. The cost of these services performed by the intermediary, however, can be excessive and should be weighed against the potential opportunity for providing the same functionalities using blockchain protocols in conjunction with a distributed ledger, instead of the intermediary.

- *Transaction maintenance*

  In a supply chain, which typically involves creating, reselling, and moving items between various parties and locations, transaction history can be extremely valuable. Transactions generated from different parties who depend on each other require a specific sequence or timing of events. If a significant number of records must be maintained without being changed, reordered, or deleted, a blockchain-based distributed ledger can provide a cost-effective alternative to maintaining transaction records centrally. Depending on the nature of the ledger, information can be made to be both transparent and publicly accessible.
- *Single-use applications*

  Single-use applications should be considered as prime candidates for initial blockchain implementation. These are likely simple and proven applications that are invisible to users and do not require changes in user behavior or processes (Iansiti & Lakhani, 2017).

  Blockchain used in conjunction with a distributed ledger and smart contract can be used to invoke low-level functions, such as existence or timestamping. It can also be embedded within ERP systems to support transactions, such as a PO, sales order, goods issue, or goods receipt, as exemplified earlier in this chapter. Procedures such as the three-way match, used for processing supplier invoices, could be carried implicitly within the blockchain protocol versus within the ERP system.
- *Digital assets*

  Assets are constantly being exchanged in a supply chain. Using serialization, assets can be tokenized in a digital form such that they can be tracked using systems. While this concept is not new, it begs the question of being able to economically track the exchange of large volumes of transactions involving those assets. Businesses that heavily rely on tracking digital assets may favor an alternative approach involving blockchain, which was purposely designed for handling tokenized assets.

Summary and conclusion

Blockchain is a new technology that securely synchronizes the same information across a distributed network of partners, such that all parties see the same thing. This avoids the need for relying on a central intermediary to validate and synchronize information and enables more information symmetry across parties. This feature alone can have profound benefits on reducing operational transaction costs, particularly in supply chain and logistics operations. Fertile areas of application include sourcing, track and trace, payment processing, logistics and shipping, supply integrity and safety, and trucking, among others.

Like many new technologies, blockchain does have caveats and may not exactly live up to hyped expectations without careful consideration. Access vulnerabilities, node and software integrity, transaction curation and validation, and lack of standards are issues that still need to be overcome. Also, early trials have shown that it is impractical to store all information regarding every transaction in a blockchain due to system and data processing constraints. Furthermore, while blockchain can eliminate functional intermediaries to handle data, other intermediaries can still exist in the form of systems and software.

Unless enterprises evolve their supply chain business and operational models, they may cease to exist. Blockchain offers an alternative for enabling newer business models by increasing efficiencies per the discussions in this chapter. Such efficiencies can improve one's ability to scale, and can help companies enrich their existing business models, move them forward, or create newer ones.

References

Caron, F. (2017). Blockchain: Identifying risk on the road to distributed ledgers. *ISACA Journal*, *5*, 24–29.

Catalini, C., & Gans, J. S. (2016). Some simple economics of blockchain. *Social Science Research Network*, 23 November.

Center for Supply Chain Studies. (2018). *DSCSA & BLOCKCHAIN Phase 2: Proof of concept*. Available from www.c4scs.org.

Galer, S. (2017). *Blockchain surge could save pharma billions*. Available from https://www.forbes.com/sites/sap/2017/12/11/blockchain-surge-could-save-pharma-billions/#7b14354c8195.

Halamka, J. D., Lippman, A., & Ekblaw, A. (2017). The potential for blockchain to transform electronic health records. *Harvard Business Review*, *3*, 1–5.

Iansiti, M., & Lakhani, K. R. (2017). The truth about blockchain. *Harvard Business Review*, *3*, 3–11.

Lohr, S., & Popper, N. (2017). *Deal book/business policy*. Available from https://www.nytimes.com/2017/03/04/business/dealbook/.

Murck, P. (2017). Who controls the blockchain. *Harvard Business Review*, April.

Nakamoto, S. (2008). *Bitcoin: A peer-to-peer electronic cash system*. Available from www.bitcoin.org.

Orcutt, M. (2017). *How blockchain could give us a smarter energy grid*. Available from https://www.technologyreview.com/s/609077/how-blockchain-could-give-us-a-smarter-energy-grid/.
Pan, M. (2016). *Blockchain: A new solution for supply integrity*. Ivey Publishing.
Sathiyamurthy, S. (2017). Design with end in mind. *ISACA Journal, 5*, 17–23.
Smith, B. (2018). *Blockchain could revolutionize the world of supply chain management*. Available from http://www.supplychainbrain.com/single-article-page/article/blockchain-could-revolutionize-the-world-of-supply-chain-management/.
Staff (2017). *New industry group looks to create blockchain standards for the freight industry*. Available from http://www.supplychainquarterly.com/news/20171108-new-industry-group-looks-to-create-blockchain-standards-for-the-freight-industry/.
Tracelink. (2015). *What is serialisation: An introduction for the life sciences supply chain*. s.n: Tracelink.
Valenta, M., & Sandner, P. (2017). *Comparison of ethereum, hyperledger fabric and corda*. Frankfurt: Frankfurt Scholl Blockchain Center.

CHAPTER 5

Technologies for dealing with error in supply chain planning

William E. Stillman
Executive Vice President and Co-owner of GAINSystems (retired)

Contents

Technology in Supply Chain Management and Logistics
DOI: https://doi.org/10.1016/B978-0-12-815956-9.00005-3

Introduction

According to the online dictionary "Wikipedia," an "error" is a deviation from accuracy or correctness. A "mistake" is an error caused by a fault: the fault being misjudgment, carelessness, or forgetfulness. So, if I run a stop sign because I was in a hurry and wasn't concentrating, and the police stop me, that is, a mistake. If, however, I try to park in an area with conflicting signs, and I get a ticket because I was incorrect on my interpretation of what the signs meant, that would be an error. The first time it would be an error. The second time it would be a mistake, since I should have known better.

Based on this definition, in most cases, we are going to be discussing technologies and techniques for dealing with "errors," not mistakes. It would be a rare occurrence for an executive to knowingly commit the same supply chain error twice, thus making it a mistake.

Murphy's law

Few will argue that one of the most challenging realities in the business world is dealing with constant change, the response to which creates an operating environment that is prone to error. Customers change their minds; raw material deliveries show up late or are short on quantity; the forecast is in error; the stocking plan is in error; and so on. Half in jest, we define the cause for all this ongoing environment of change as "Murphy's law": "Whatever can go wrong, will go wrong." Although we expend great efforts in trying to minimize the negative financial impacts of "Murphy's law," we have not been successful in eliminating it or effectively managing it as far as supply chain plans are concerned. For most companies, we accommodate it in practice by enabling inventory write-offs, physical and financial buffers, and setting up actual budgets to accommodate the prescribed cost of expediting.

All of these accommodations and buffers are based on a plan, as is almost everything in business. To control the business against a finite amount of money, we set up production plans, inventory policies, replenishment plans, distribution plans, and so on. Then we try to manage the business to these plans effectively. Unfortunately, error gets in our way. We miss our targeted plans and either spend more money trying to correct for "Murphy" and miss earning more money because "Murphy" results in lost orders.

As with anything in the business world, if you want to achieve targeted objectives and do so in a certain time frame, against defined specifications, under predetermined conditions, with a maximum contribution to margin, you need to create a plan that you can not only follow, but one where you can control and/or manage the error (aka, "Murphy"). Managing a company's supply chain is no different.

Simply put, a corporate supply chain is that flow of inventory or goods that delivers a requested product to a customer on the day requested in the size, shape, color, and so on, the customer requested. The ultimate goal in this process is to achieve the "perfect order," that order, which meets all customer parameters and specifications, is delivered exactly as requested and maximizes the contribution to the supplier's margin.

This issue has challenged the executive suite for years. Corporations have spent hundreds of millions of dollars on outside consulting firms and enterprise software trying to manage the impact of "Murphy" on their inventory investment and operating costs. All to no avail. According to the 2015 Annual State of the Logistics Report issued by the Council of Supply Chain Management Professionals (CSCMP, 2015), the inventory-to-sales ratio, which measures a business' inventory investment in relation to its monthly sales, rose rapidly in 2014. The ratio ended in 2014 at 1.35, its highest level since late 2009. A rising ratio generally indicates declining sales or excess inventory levels. What is even more interesting is that from 2000 to 2009, according to the US Census Bureau, Department of Commerce, the ratio had remained essentially flat, oscillating between 1.4 and 1.3 (CSCMP, 2015).

ERP software

According to Gartner Group (2018), in the last 20 years, we have also seen the greatest growth in history in the purchase of enterprise planning and operational software investment. All of that investment in tools intended to improve return on inventory investment or operational efficiency; and yet, little, if any, average industry improvement has been documented (specific companies may have documented improvement, but on average manufacturers received little return on investment from their software and consulting project investments).

The reason for this is twofold. In order to deal with the complexities of "Murphy," the corporate and the consulting world segmented the overall problem into what they perceived as "manageable" pieces and built projects and methods around each piece. There was a project for solving the forecasting issues, another project for solving the demand planning issues, another project for warehousing issues, another for the distribution network, another one for production, and so on. What no one recognized at the time was that the problem could not be optimally solved in silos. The reason is that silos or various parts were interdependent and therefore needed to be solved simultaneously, across the enterprise.

The second challenge, related to such interdependence, is that no one had tools that could support resolution of an enterprise-wide problem where the interdependence of so many variables required the simultaneous, comprehensive analysis and resolution, in an environment that was constantly changing. The segmented silo approach, by its very nature, added incremental error to the enterprise problem as a whole, thus further ensuring more error. More error correlates to more cost.

Remember, all of this effort and expense is expended in an effort for management to achieve the "Perfect Order."

Inventory planning by stock-keeping unit level for every location

In order to consistently achieve the "Perfect Order," with the maximum contribution to margin, one needs to plan across the enterprise at the most granular level. This means planning at the item or stock-keeping unit (SKU) level for every location (SKUL) where inventory is held or used. In some of his original research on inventory behavior in the supply chain, Prof. William C. Benton of Purdue University realized that every SKUL in an enterprise can have a unique pattern of behavior and that pattern of behavior changes at least once in a 10- to 14-week period. He further realized that in no two such periods will such change take place at the same time.

As Prof. Benton continued his research, he also recognized that if one were to establish a plan to consistently achieve the "Perfect Order," one needed to account in that plan for all variables and needed to monitor the enterprise to identify any changes in SKUL behavior patterns, customer behavior patterns, or other relevant elements of the enterprise supply chain. In addition, one needed to forecast and plan around comprehensive error and variability with the objective of being able to manage that comprehensive error.

These two discoveries, the need to forecast and analyze at the SKUL level across the enterprise and the need to plan and manage comprehensive error and variability including all costs, constraints, dependencies, and so on, formed the foundation of the Science of Inventory Optimization (IO) for which Prof. Benton was one of the early practitioners.

As Julie Fraser (2016) of Iyno Advisors, a global operations and strategy consulting firm, has recognized:

> *To become a world class trading partner in today's environment of change and uncertainty requires an organization to be diligent and proactive in real time planning. Only companies that can effectively plan and manage their supply chain can reach their full financial potential. With change becoming the new constant, supply chain planning is critical; companies must build a full-time center of excellence that can deliver plans and updates in real time.*

That said, even the best supply chain plans often do not achieve their objectives. The colloquial quip, "stuff happens," is all too often part of the executive vernacular. The primary reason these plans are not met is that the planning methods and tools used do not get granular enough nor are they able to monitor dynamically and replan in real time.

> *The division of labor that has worked until now—such as demand, inventory, or production planning—has actually impeded the ability to optimize because optimization needs to fully and concurrently consider impacts across every SKU in every location in every phase of the supply chain. Our brains are not wired to handle that, but fortunately some software developers have been able to create dynamic tools and suites of algorithms that follow the rules and principles of the Science of Inventory Optimization, states Julie Fraser of Iyno Advisors Frazer (2016).*

Science of inventory optimization

The Science of IO ensures supply chain plans are both profit-optimized and as highly accurate as possible. Error is minimized to near zero.

To do this, leading-edge science of IO solutions treat the supply chain as one, contiguous, homogeneous entity. It is not broken up into silos or fiefdoms that operate uniquely and can therefore only be planned uniquely and then, through some form of collaboration, fused together. The Science states: all elements/ components of the enterprise are interdependent and linked. *You cannot affect demand without affecting supply. You cannot affect replenishments without affecting costs. You cannot affect inventory policies without impacting customer orders, and so on.* The Science of IO envelops every aspect of the enterprise where any piece of inventory rests or passes through. When management plans to deliver the "Perfect Order," it needs to incorporate, comprehensively, every element of the enterprise simultaneously. This is because every component of the enterprise, down to the smallest SKUL, is subject to change at any time. Therefore to consistently achieve the "Perfect Order," management needs to comprehensively monitor, analyze, and plan all policies, plans, and actions for the enterprise, at every SKUL level, every day.

Today's leading-edge ERP solutions already capture some 95% of the data required for IO. Cutting-edge IO solutions quickly and efficiently interface with such ERP solutions and collect and format any data that may still be missing from the ERP solution.

To this point, we have talked about the capability of the Science of IO at a high level. Let us look at a more granular level as to some of the more specific functionalities a profit-optimized IO solution needs to have in order to achieve the profit optimal "Perfect Order."

The science of inventory optimization components for planning a perfect order

Optimized demand planning and forecasting

Forecasting is not a new concept to most of us. Its basics are well known. We take a period of time as our historical base, run that curve against a forecasting model, and derive an expected demand pattern against which we try to project tomorrow's demand. What the Science of IO has identified is that such granular forecasting is difficult to achieve without a supportive IO tool.

Additionally, forecasting cannot be a standalone functionally. It needs to be an integral part of an entire IO tool, a tool that dynamically:

1. Forecasts at the lowest level: SKUL
2. Recognizes that every SKUL can change its pattern of behavior at least once every 14 months.
3. Recognizes that in no two periods does a pattern of behavior change at the same time.

4. Given the number of potential patterns of behavior possible, one needs to be able to select from some 40 or more forecast models to ensure that all potential behavior patterns are covered.
5. In order to achieve all these, given the thousands of items (SKULs) most companies have in their operations, this needs to be done dynamically.
6. Given the potential frequency of pattern change, it also needs to be redone whenever a pattern change is detected that could have a financially significant impact on the company.
7. The resulting forecasts need to be tested dynamically for plausibility—how well does the forecast fit the current and expected economic conditions? When conditions or behavior patterns change, what is the impact on the plan, costs, policies, and the total enterprise?

Pattern-recognition models

In the manufacturing and distribution sectors, there are more than 40 pattern-recognition models that might map to a specific SKUL's pattern of behavior. These need to be incorporated into the planning and optimization tool so that they automatically recognize any pattern changes and dynamically predict a revised baseline for the future demand that matches the predicted new pattern.

In his original research, Prof. Benton built a dynamic model testing and selection process (early artificial intelligence and machine learning) that evaluated about 110 potential models. The goal was to find that model, for each SKUL that provided the most plausible or best manageable demand pattern. Minimizing error was not the goal. Contrary to popular belief, in an optimized environment, the objective is not necessarily to pick the model that provides the least error, but rather to pick the model that most effectively enables the management of the error and its associated costs.

The dynamic IO solution that Prof. Benton invented, called General Adaptive Inventory Solution, dynamically evaluates a suite of over 40 potential forecast models in relationship to all other relevant variables and economic conditions (Fig. 5.1).

Planning with comprehensive error

We have already addressed the concept of comprehensive error to some degree. As is detailed in the following chart, there is significantly more

Proven forecast model library

- 40 proven forecast models —11 categories
- Dynamically runs models for every SKUL
- Dynamically performs validation tests
- Dynamically simulates for plausibility
- Ensures forecast error is manageable
- Manageable error is the foundation for Profit Optimized Inventory Policy (facilitated through the use of machine learning and AI)

Family	Description
I	Straight line/moving average
II	Zero or simple trend/seasonal
III	Exponential smoothing
IV	Linear regression
V	Double exponential smoothing
VI	Significant trend/seasonal
VII	Low volume
VIII	Sporadic poisson distribution
IX	Low volume poisson distribution
X	Effort based models (service parts)
XI	Attribute based models

Figure 5.1 Dynamic model selection to support optimal forecasting.

Need to plan for comprehensive error

Based on a study of 50 manufacturing companies, comparing actual inventory counts to both planned and stated count, GAINSystems, Inc found these typical errors to exist at all companies.

PIPE	PIPE Units	Typical % error	Unit error	UNIT error range
Onhand	70	+/- 3%	+/- 2	
Replenishment orders	120	+/- 11%	+/- 13	
Un-shipped	-10	+/- 10%	+/- 1	
Forecast demand	-100	+/- 50%	+/- 50	82% of total unit error
Service stock	-30	+/- 80%	+/- 24	is in FD and SS
PIPE value	50		+/- 90	+140 to -40

Figure 5.2 Planning with comprehensive error.

error in an enterprise than the traditional forecast error, which most leading-edge, ERP-based planning systems focus on as a silo. In order to plan a profit optimal, "Perfect Order," one needs to identify, analyze, and measure comprehensive error for every SKUL simultaneously across the enterprise (Fig. 5.2).

Now introduce a new product. How will this change tomorrow's demand pattern? How do you now plan for tomorrow's production? In all probability, the policies and plans now need to adjust dynamically for an upward trend in demand while the phase-out of a mature product will show a decline in demand. These patterns of behavior need to be anticipated to assure that the inventory investment is optimal.

Once you have achieved a profit optimal demand plan or forecast, you need to translate that into the profit optimal supply chain plan. This incorporates not only the demand plan, but also the replenishment plan, distribution plan, production plan, and so on. Remember that all of these elements are integral to the delivery of the "Perfect Order."

Additional essential capabilities of a world-class inventory optimization solution

Leading indicator analysis

This analysis automatically determines likely shifts in historical demand patterns and auto-adjusts the baseline forecast; these leading indicators can include such information as machine/fleet usage data in the equipment repair sector. Example indicators include:

- macroeconomic indicators such as changes in housing starts, interest rates, and vehicle purchases;
- commodity price changes; and
- point-of-sale data.

In many cases, issues not directly associated with historical demand patterns may influence future demand. For example, a company may open additional distribution centers requiring additional inventory investment not anticipated in the historical demand patterns. A company that sells to the building products industry may be influenced by factors such as anticipated housing starts or interest rates or both. Anticipating these kinds of changes can help develop an optimal inventory plan to support the anticipated changes in demand. Examples can be found in Chapter 9, Case studies of supply chain technology implementation.

"New-item" management

"New-item" management is used for superseding (direct replacements), similar (mostly similar attributes), related (some similar attributes), and entirely new product launches.

The introduction of new products presents additional challenges because no historical demand patterns may exist for demand planning purposes. New items can be replacements for existing products, in which case the patterns of demand for the replaced part can be used as a guide to initiate the plan for the new part. The other extreme is where the product is entirely new. In this case, an estimated pattern of demand can be used to initiate the plan and then is closely monitored (dynamically) as the actual demand is captured. All of this needs to be done while simultaneously including the behavior patterns and costs associated with the other points in this list.

Cross-department and cross-enterprise collaboration

Collaboration can be used to include "extrinsic" or market knowledge into the forecast (that cannot effectively be captured via Leading Indicators). This includes:

- Ability to manage workflow across multiple groups in the organization (e.g., marketing, sales, finance, operations).
- Ability to share demand (or replenishment) plans with suppliers and customers for notification, validation, and refinement.

This functionality provides for the inclusion of market-type knowledge, which is not available through leading indicator analysis. It also provides for input from company organizations such as marketing (e.g., promotions), sales (e.g., price changes), operations (e.g., plant shutdown), and so on. The system then also provides for sharing the resulting demand plans with suppliers and customers to properly communicate anticipated results.

Multiechelon stocking policy optimization

These are algorithms that determine whether to stock an item and at what service level to stock each item, based on:

- impact on total costs or profit or both;
- interdependencies among locations (at the same or different levels in the network);
- interdependencies within a bill-of-material (BOM), such as where-used, density, critical path likelihood, cumulative lead-time, and so on, to devise "postponement strategies"; and
- customer expectations.

There are a number of factors that influence what, where, and in what quantities to stock. This functionality takes into consideration the service-level objective as well as the cost-optimal service level, cost, and profit impact of stocking policy, product interdependencies between stocking locations, interdependencies within a BOM including where-used dependencies, critical path likelihood, cumulative lead-time, and so on, and customer expectations (e.g., stocking minimums).

Inventory policy optimization

This considers a comprehensive set of planning error sources to identify the optimal ordering sizes and buffer stock including consistently achieved targeted service levels. These error sources include, at a minimum:

- demand plan/forecast error;
- lead-time variation;
- yield/quantity-delivered performance; and
- optimal ordering cycles (considering ordering constraints as well as price breaks).

In order to develop the optimal reorder quantity, this functionality considers a variety of factors. These include the forecast/demand plan error, lead-time variation (the difference between when the product was expected vs when it was received), yield/quantity received variation (quantity ordered vs quantity received), as well as ordering constraints (when will product be available). In addition, price breaks (the more ordered, the less the unit cost but the higher the carrying cost) are also considered. See the Benco case in Chapter 9, Case studies of supply chain technology implementation.

Service-level optimization

This capability automatically and uniquely determines the service level needed for each item to achieve the aggregate target service level while minimizing or maximizing a business objective. For example:

- determining the mix of service levels by item to deliver total service level of 98% with minimum inventory investment and
- determining the mix of service levels by item to deliver maximum service while maintaining a specific inventory investment, inventory turnover, or purchasing budget.

In addition to determining the inventory investment required to meet service-level objectives, this functionality can establish the mix of service levels by item to attain an overall service-level objective, as well as determine the mix of service levels by item to achieve a specific inventory investment, inventory turnover target, or purchasing budget. See the section on steel pipe and supply in Chapter 9, Case studies of supply chain technology implementation.

Routing (i.e., network-flow) optimization

Routing optimization considers which supplier provides the lowest total cost and, in multisite environments, how to plan the flow of product through the network that considers:

- the inventory savings of hub-and-spoke (via buffer-stock pooling) and
- the rehandling and transportation cost savings of direct-from-supplier shipping.

There are some hybrid advantages of "cross-dock" logistics. In multisite environments, this functionality plans the flow of product through the distribution network considering potential inventory savings with a hub-and-spoke environment, potential benefits with direct-from-supplier shipping, and potential advantages of "cross-dock" logistics (reconciling differences between potential demand, when product is ordered, vs actual demand, when product is received). Steel service centers find this functionality of great value in optimizing shipments from large vendors who have minimum purchase requirements for their distribution.

Sourcing optimization

Determines the supplier(s) that provide the lowest total cost considering:

- ordering minimums and volume discounts (line and cross-item/order level) considering the level of demand;
- inbound logistics costs;
- lead-time and lead-time performance; and
- procurement costs.

Where multiple suppliers for the same part(s) are available (e.g., local vs offshore), this functionality helps determine which supplier(s) provide the lowest total cost considering minimum order sizes and volume discounts, inbound logistics costs, lead-time variability costs, and procurement costs. Several uniform suppliers in the United States use this functionality to balance their offshore and domestic suppliers, preferring the offshore due to cost but maintaining local sources to accommodate volatile demand requirements.

Key capabilities of a world-class replenishment optimization solution

New order creation, prioritization, and auto-approval

The order creation process should consider lead-time requirements, the likelihood of stock out, optimized order quantities, and auto-approval risks versus benefits. This functionality generates the production/purchase order for the previously calculated optimal order quantity and can consider lead-time requirements and risks versus benefits of auto-approval when the product arrives.

Transfer order prioritization and creation

Transfer order prioritization considers parent–child, for example, headquarters–division relationships and, in instances of shortage, allocates as needed to minimize risk-of-stock out. This function considers the parent–child relationship of ordered parts and will reallocate as needed to minimize the risk-of-stock outs.

Optimized redistribution

Redistribution will optimally consider carrying costs of excess as well as on-order inventory to preclude new supply orders when unnecessary. This approach considers the cost of excess stock as well as on-order stock to preclude the processing of new supply orders when not necessary.

Optimized component allocation

In instances of component shortages, the optimal approach allocates components to multiple later-stage items to minimize finished goods stock outs across the entire network (i.e., allocation optimized across multiple echelons). In situations where there are shortages of components, this functionality will allocate the available components to those items that are in later stages of assembly in order to minimize finished goods (and costlier) stock outs.

Cross-dock optimization

With the ability to redetermine target locations dynamically for inbound supplies to the hub location, the "cross-dock" function optimally reconciles the difference between target demand locations for a product when it was ordered versus the current demand locations when the product is received. Because of the multiple stocking locations and high service-level requirements, Mayer Electric has found this functionality of key value.

Rotables planning optimization (Maintenance, Repair and Operations/warranty)

Rotables are parts that can be rebuilt or overhauled. The optimal approach considers unique repair parts planning needs such as:

- core/carcass reverse logistics;
- variable repair times;
- capacity constraints;
- repair yields and requirements to "refresh" the rotable pool with new purchases;
- potential "zero-sum" rotable pool constraints/parameters; and
- compliance with performance-based logistics requirements, which is an outcomes-based product support strategy.

A major market opportunity for IO is repair parts planning. Some of the unique requirements of this industry include the planning of the repair/rotable items, also termed core/carcass reverse logistics. Some of the variables for which IO plans include variable repair times based on what requires fixing, capacity constraints where a production center is also used for repair work, and the need to replenish the rotable inventory pool with new purchases.

Automated and optimized order pooling

Optimal order pooling dynamically builds multiitem and potentially multilocation orders that minimize the cost related to meeting supplier constraints (e.g., minimum value and full container). Where replenishment planning can include multiple items for multiple locations all from the same vendors, this functionality builds multiple item/location orders to take advantage of supplier constraints, including minimum value, full container, and so on.

Optimized expediting and de-expediting

This functionality considers the costs/benefits of actions to focus attention on high-impact actions often obscured by low-value-added "noise." This functionality provides focus and priority to those actions that have high benefits in relation to costs to keep them from being obscured by low-value-added "noise." For example, if you are expecting product from an offshore source in 6 weeks, and the demand for that product has been rescheduled to a future period, this functionality will determine whether it makes sense to incur the cost of rescheduling the incoming product versus bringing it in as scheduled and incurring the additional carrying cost.

"Rough-cut" production capacity optimization

This "rough-cut" functionality optimally smooths orders in light of prebuild when needed (e.g., in seasonal environments) and allocates projected needs optimally during shortages. This functionality helps "balance" production requirements for those periods when capacity is available and cost-optimally allocates capacity for those periods where there are excess demands. This function is often used in situations of highly seasonal business and limited production capacity; this functionality can be used to optimize manufacturing of product during the "off-season" so it is available during the peak season.

Cycled production management

Cycled production management optimizes inventory policy and ordering in light of fixed ordering cycles (e.g., batched production runs). Related functionalities are purchase order manager, supplier planning porter, and supplier scorecard.

The purchase order manager facilitates web-based communication of initial orders as well as subsequent changes (expedite and de-expedite requests) in a prioritized and value-driven fashion.

This functionality supports web-based communication to suppliers of new orders (both purchasing as well as manufacturing) as well as changes (including expedite/de-expedite) to existing orders in a prioritized and value-driven fashion. In this manner, those items that are critical appear "at the top of the list."

Supplier planning portal provides configurable and secure requirements forecasts to ensure supplier readiness and improved delivery performance (to drive lower costs for both parties). Configurable requirements forecasts can be provided to suppliers (both purchasing as well as manufacturing) to give the supplier a "peek" at anticipated requirements that can then be used to help them in their planning, thus resulting in improved supplier readiness and delivery performance.

Supplier scorecard provides detailed and objective performance measures in both absolute and relative (i.e., ranking) terms, including estimating cost impacts of performance issues. This function provides the ability to measure supplier performance, including yield (quantity of products ordered vs received) as well as delivery (when products ordered vs when received). This information can then show the cost impact of performance issues (i.e., how much additional inventory and at what cost) has to be carried to accommodate poor supplier performance.

Operational questions your inventory and replenishment optimization solutions should be able to answer dynamically

Purchasing/supplier management—typical issues/applications

Here are some of the key operational questions your inventory and replenishment optimization solutions should be able to answer dynamically:

1. Which supplier ensures my lowest cost operations considering: Standard costs?
2. Supply yield variance?
3. Actual lead-time variance?
4. Is this opportunistic volume discount truly profitable?
5. What does this shipping delay cost me in added operational expense?
6. What does this shipping delay cost me in customer service delay?
7. Considering profit and customer service, with which vendor should I place this order to ensure we meet customer requests at the lowest cost?
8. What is my best mix of vendors, where I have multiple sources, to ensure that I hit targeted customer service levels and yet still maximize my contribution to profit?

Purchasing/replenishment planning—typical issues/applications

Typical purchasing and replenishment questions relating to planning and applications include:

1. What size order quantity should I place to ensure that the company meets promised service levels?
2. What size order quantity should I place to ensure that the company operates at least cost?
3. When should I place the next order to ensure meeting company profit goals?
4. What size shipping container should I request for least-cost operations?

5. Which orders should I consolidate to ensure lowest cost achievement of promised customer deliveries?
6. How can I consolidate orders in order to minimize transportation costs and still ensure that my promised customer delivery dates are met 99.9% of the time?
7. When I order from my offshore supplier, am I required to order in full container loads? How do I determine what is the profit optimal container mix for future demand when I have to calculate in volume?
8. When being required to order in full container loads or full truckloads, and I do not have an immediate need for a full load, how do I pull in expected future orders by cost and volume?

Inventory planning and management—typical issues/applications

Questions to be answered when performing inventory planning and management include:

1. How much space will be needed over the next 6–12 months for least-cost operations?
2. What is the least-cost stocking location for item "X" to ensure promised delivery?
3. Considering all costs (transport, setups, expediting, etc.), what is the least-cost stocking plan, by location, to provide my targeted customer fill rate, all line items?
4. Which items are most cost-effectively stocked as subassemblies?
5. Which items are most cost-effectively handled as "cross-dock" items?
6. My company continues to grow; where should I put my next warehouse? What size should it be? What items should be stocked there? What impact does this have on my current locations and stocking plans?

Manufacturing/production—typical issues/applications

Manufacturing and production questions include:

1. What is my most cost-effective manufacturing lot size over the next 6 months?
2. How do I achieve the lowest setup costs while ensuring that targeted customer service levels are achieved against customer delivery dates?
3. How do I plan labor utilization against demand to ensure cost optimization?

4. Given current capacity, what should I manufacture and when to maximize profit?
5. Given my very seasonal demand and my capacity over the next 6 months, when and how many of each product should I manufacture to ensure I meet demand, don't create back orders, and ensure least-cost operations?
6. To compensate for seasonal demand, what should I manufacture now when I have excess capacity to ensure maximized profit and no future stock outs?

Financial issues/applications—typical issues/applications

1. How much cash do I need to budget over the next XX quarters to support my inventory investment requirements?
2. What are the incremental costs that will be incurred each month due to supplier delivery delays or yield issues?
3. What are the incremental costs in expediting and inventory investment caused by capacity constraints?
4. Given expected sales growth, at what point do the incremental expediting costs and inventory investment costs warrant adding manufacturing or warehouse capacity?
5. What expenses can be reduced by consolidating our planning and purchasing into a centralized function?
6. What are our earnings improvements obtained by profit optimizing our distribution network?
7. What is the negative cash drain (cost) of allowing customer-dedicated inventory levels now that we can document a guaranteed customer service level?

Marketing and sales—typical issues/applications

1. What is my profit-maximized customer service level for my "A" customers?
2. How does this customer's request for faster delivery impact profit margins?
3. If I use "service" as a strategic tool to win market share, what will it cost?
4. Does the value of lost sales at current customer service levels compare to the total costs of increasing service levels warrant trying to capture those lost sales?

5. Which region, customer, type of customer, and so on, costs the least to service?
6. How will a change in customer requirements impact our service level?
7. Given our current expected customer orders, what is the impact on our margins of offering this customer premium service?
8. What would the impact be on delivery if this customer changed their order?
9. I have an emergency customer need; how can I deliver this product at the least cost and still meet my customer's emergency delivery date?

References

Council of Supply Chain Management Professionals (CSCMP). (2015). 27th Annual State of the Logistics Report. <https://cscmp.org/>.

Gartner Group. (2018). Market Guide for Supply Chain Analytics Technology, 2018, Noha Tohamy (Ed.), April 5.

Interview With Julie Frasier. (2016). Iyno Advisors, 31 Capt. Murphy's Way, Cummaquid, MA.

Further reading

Archives of GAIN Systems, Inc. 1200 N. Ashland Avenue, Chicago, IL.

CHAPTER 6

Emerging technologies in the health-care supply chain

JoAnn Verdin
Parkinson School of the Health Sciences and Public Health, Department of Healthcare Administration, Loyola University Chicago, Chicago, IL, United States

Contents

Introduction

The health-care system is moving from centralized, hospital-based care to a more decentralized model, including outpatient options such as ambulatory surgery centers, mobile clinics, and telemedicine (Landro, 2018). With these changes comes the need to utilize new strategies in the supply chain to make sure the right supplies, devices, and pharmaceuticals are

Technology in Supply Chain Management and Logistics
DOI: https://doi.org/10.1016/B978-0-12-815956-9.00006-5

available throughout the health-care system. The use of new technologies will be required to meet these changing needs as well as to streamline the supply chain throughout the system.

Background

Supply-chain management has taken on an increasingly important role in health care. The need to operate efficiently and decrease costs in an environment of high deductible health plans and decreasing reimbursement from payers has resulted in greater reliance on supply-chain management.

1965–83

Medicare and Medicaid were established in 1965 (Shi & Singh, 2017, pp. 69–70). Until 1983, inpatient facilities, including hospitals and nursing homes, were reimbursed on a retrospective basis. This meant that the previous year's costs were used to determine the next year's reimbursement. In this environment, there was little emphasis on controlling the costs of purchasing and materials management within hospitals or other long-term care facilities. Centralized management in these areas did develop during this time due to increasing expenses (Shi & Singh, 2017; Wolper, 2011).

1980s and 1990s

In 1983 Medicare began using a prospective reimbursement plan where preestablished criteria were used to determine the amount of reimbursement for specific services. No longer was reimbursement based on previous costs but was determined by diagnostic related groups for Medicare Part A in 1983, and since 2000 ambulatory payment classifications, resource utilization groups, and home health resource groups have been used. The importance of lowering supply-chain costs and increasing efficiency was emphasized (Shi & Singh, 2017, pp. 158–160).

During the 1980s and 1990s, emphasis was placed on developing group purchasing organizations. These are defined as "an organization whose primary product or service is the development of purchasing contracts with product and nonlabor service vendors that its members can access" (Burns, 2002, p. 60; Schneller & Smeltzer, 2006). In addition, the centralized management of inventories and reliance on supplier services evolved.

2000s

During the 2000s, there was a consolidation of supply-chain functions resulting in increased efficiency. This was also a time when many hospitals, outpatient facilities, and physicians' offices merged, resulting in the potential for centralization of supply chain and distribution services. For example, Intermountain Healthcare has centralized all aspects of its supply chain into four areas of operations: category management, purchasing, logistics and materials management, support services, and business programs and services. This represents a change away from the traditional health-care organizations' reliance on external suppliers (Intermountain Healthcare).

Typical organization of the health-care supply chain

The health-care supply chain must meet three critical elements (Wolper, 2011, p. 574):

1. Corporate strategy ensuring materials (i.e., goods, services, and equipment) are purchased at the lowest total cost. This includes factors outside the actual price. The cost of acquisition, shipping, storing, using, and replacing is all part of the total cost.
2. There must be a strategy to ensure inventories and their associated carrying costs are aggressively monitored and controlled. Many items in the supply chain have expiration dates that must be respected. Pharmaceuticals, for example, cannot be used after they expire, so it is important that the supplies kept in inventory are utilized prior to expiration.
3. A system is needed for ensuring the ready availability of all required materials. The goal is to have the supplies at the location where they are needed so everything is used before it expires and direct patient caregivers do not spend time looking for supplies. There must be sufficient supplies on hand for normal use and a plan in case of emergencies. This includes blood, pharmaceuticals, medical supplies, and laboratory supplies to collect samples. There also must be a process to obtain surgical supplies and medical devices when needed.

In a hospital or ambulatory surgery center, all the departments are internal to or contracted by the organization except the supplier. The supplier could be the original manufacturer, a group purchasing organization, or a third-party supplier.

Communications among the departments are essential to reduce the total cost of supplies. It is important that the essential details regarding the purchase of goods and services, the terms of delivery, when these are received, where these are stored, and when these are used can be determined. Once used, this information may go back to the originating department so that it can be reordered.

This process applies to pharmaceuticals, medical supplies, and medical devices. Other items and services purchased also must be tracked to make sure they are available when needed and that all items and services have been received.

Originating departments

The process begins with originating departments in the health-care system. The requirements related to the supply chain must be coordinated, so each has what is required to care for patients directly or to support the care of patients indirectly.

Surgical services include orthopedics, cardiology, and many other surgical areas. This area requires expensive surgical supplies, instruments, and medical devices. In order to minimize the total cost of supplies for this area, it would make sense to standardize the medical devices used for the same procedures. However, physician preferences may result in medical devices being ordered from multiple sources. Many organizations have formed value analysis teams that include all stakeholders to review purchases to see where standardization and potential cost savings are possible. This area also houses the sterile reprocessing department with special equipment and supplies needed to sterilize everything used during surgery. Because of the high cost and complexity found in surgical services, there is often a supply-chain director or manager in charge of this area.

Obstetrical services include areas for normal deliveries, cesarean sections as well as a neonatal intensive care unit. Each of these requires specialized supplies and equipment for its patients. Just as in surgical services, the instruments used must be sterilized by the sterile reprocessing department and be ready for the next patient.

Oncology, cardiology, general medicine, and intensive care units all have different requirements in terms of equipment and pharmaceuticals used. The organization's supply-chain management must stock standard supplies as well as specialized items as needed.

Allied health departments include professionals from occupational, physical, and speech therapy, diagnostic departments including X-ray, nuclear medicine, and ultrasound as well as radiation therapy. These areas also have specialized needs for equipment to provide diagnoses or therapy. Diagnostic radiology also may use contrast materials and radiopharmaceuticals. These must be managed and disposed of according to the procedures outlined by the hospital as well as regulators.

Laboratories and pharmacies have specific needs throughout the supply chain. It is important that samples and pharmaceuticals are maintained at specific temperatures from the time they are shipped to when they are delivered to the time they are used.

Support areas include the ordering, preparation, and delivery of food to patients and having clean linens available. Supplies are also needed for cleaning, disinfecting, and maintaining the environment as well as tools and equipment to repair the many systems in the organization.

Administrative areas require office and computer supplies and equipment. There may be training and meeting facilities that have audiovisual equipment that must be maintained either internally or as part of a maintenance contract.

The information technology department has become central to a health-care system's operations. Computers in various forms are found throughout a hospital and in outpatient areas (ambulatory surgical centers, physician offices, and immediate care centers). Administrative systems are used for scheduling and billing, delivering, tracking staff education, and providing patient access to their information. These are also used for purchasing, receiving, storing, and distributing supplies and equipment throughout a facility. Clinical systems ideally include patient information from the physician offices, outpatient departments, and inpatient units. The information from all these systems can be fed into a central data warehouse to be analyzed for studies supporting medical research and operations. Security of the equipment itself, as well as all of the data in these systems, is part of the IT department's role.

Purchasing department

The purchasing department interfaces with originating departments and the suppliers (group purchasing organization, individual manufacturer, or third-party supplier.) For large contracts, there is usually a Request for Proposal sent to potential suppliers, and the evaluation committee uses this information plus meetings with the "finalists" to determine who wins the contract. The goal is to achieve the best total cost for the products or services. This includes the procurement cost, product cost, and management cost.

Supplier

Group purchasing organizations, manufacturers, and third-party logistics providers for medical supplies and pharmaceuticals may all provide supplies to a large health system. Contracts may also exist with suppliers of linens, food services, environmental services, and waste management.

There are different arrangements with suppliers. The goal is that the health-care organization needs to ensure it has all supplies, medical devices, pharmaceuticals, etc., needed at all times. Depending on the size of the system, the requirements will vary.

Receiving

The receiving department receives the items, checks the orders, and enters that the items have been received into the computer system. The items are then sent to the inventory/distribution department. If receiving is located in a central warehouse, items might need to be delivered to each facility's inventory/distribution department and then distributed to the end users.

Certain supplies and drugs must be kept at a certain temperature. Are parts of the delivery cart temperature controlled? If not, how do you ensure they are kept at the correct temperature throughout the facilities' supply chain?

Sometimes the order is delivered directly to the originating department by the supplier. This may be especially true for a nonclinical department since their needs do not overlap with the materials received in the clinical system. They also need to record the delivery in the appropriate system.

Inventory/distribution system

Inventory management within the organization is an important part of reducing total costs. To manage inventory, a typical approach is to determine what is there and how fast inventory is used. Slow-moving inventory can be returned for credit, used by another department, donated, or sold. Then, determine the reorder points and economic order quantity, do an inventory count, and determine the progress. This may also be automated in an inventory system. For example, if the electronic medical record (EMR) is connected to the inventory in the pharmacy, the physician order for the medication can "deduct" it from the total count in the pharmacy, and it will be sent to the unit. The nurse then gives the medication to the patient and scans that it has been used into the EMR. The central system will then have a new inventory count.

A number of approaches might be used to distribute supplies from a facilities central storeroom. Requisitions from the originating departments may be used to place orders on an ad hoc basis. Since the orders may be placed randomly, too much or too little stock may be kept in the central location or on the originating department. There also may be last-minute orders. Rather than relying on a system that predicts usage based on past experience, so the area is properly stocked, an ad hoc approach is used in many medical facilities.

Exchange carts may be used to take the basic supplies needed to and from the storeroom to the point of use. If a duplicate cart is prepared, then the loading process is centralized and the carts are exchanged on a regular basis. This, however, results in duplication of supplies and the need to store the "backup" cart in the facility.

Surgical carts are also prepared for each surgery, containing the instruments and supplies that will be used. They can be stored outside of the operating room itself in a nearby location. Once the surgery is over, the cart and all of the instruments can be returned to the sterile reprocessing area. This ensures that the instruments are all taken for reprocessing.

Preauthorized replenishment-level (PAR-level) systems are maintained by individuals from the central storeroom. They visit each area regularly and determine what supplies need to be replenished. This may be done with a scanner or be part of an automated inventory system. These orders are then filled and the material replenished in the department. Computer systems might supplement the counting function by predicting future use based on past utilization. The predicted order is then delivered.

The point-of-use system is similar to that used by retailers. The caregiver enters or scans the code of the item used into the EMR, the inventory is reduced, and the information needed for charge capture is recorded. The system can then trigger an order for the items to be replenished. Unique identifiers on medical devices are also entered into the system. If it is necessary to recall the device at a later date, the patient who received it can be identified.

The items could be delivered by self-driving robots or by the central receiving staff. There are also potential efficiencies if the receiving staff also puts them away rather than the clinical staff in the unit. Pharmacy techs may deliver the medications to the drug dispensing cabinet in the unit (Vecchione, 2017, pp. 19–20) and put them into the patient's drawers. The dispensing units should be connected to the EMR system and delivery recorded in the system.

Accounts payable

Accounts payable is part of the finance department in most organizations. The staff work with the departments that receive the orders to make sure invoices are paid on time, and there are no late fees. The process is automated so that everyone can determine what has been received and make sure the invoices are paid according to the contract. Originating department budgets may be charged if the items are not part of the clinical process. This is especially true for administrative departments and other nonclinical support areas.

Impact of new technologies on the health-care supply chain

Utilizing the framework outlined in Chapter 2, Technologies in supply-chain management and logistics, the current and potential role of these technologies will be discussed. In some cases the technologies are applied to the delivery of health care, and there is a resulting change in the supply-chain requirements.

Maturing technologies

These technologies are appropriate for large group purchasing organizations, suppliers, and 3PLs, as well as in health-care facilities themselves.

Optimization software is used by Benco Dental (see Chapter 5: Technologies for dealing with error in supply-chain planning) to reduce inventory, increase market share and sales, and eliminate expedited shipments.

Sensors/telematics, such as RFID, are available for expensive, mobile equipment throughout the facility. Many pharmaceuticals must be kept below a certain temperature so sensors throughout the supply chain may be used. Telematics can also be used for vehicle fleets delivering supplies to and from a central warehouse. In addition, medical devices have unique identifiers that are scanned into the patient's EMR so he/she can be contacted if an upgrade or recall is needed (Endicott, 2017).

Cloud computing allows all appropriate parties access to the data and provides storage for the large amounts of data housed in EMRs and administrative systems. Security of the data is paramount as health-care facilities have been targeted by hackers and have paid ransoms to "release" their patient data. The Health Insurance Portability and Accountability Act is a US law that protects patients' medical records and other health information provided to health plans, doctors, hospitals, and other health-care providers. The US Department of Health and Human Services outlines specific regulations related to the security of cloud storage for Personal Health Information (PHI) (Guidance on HIPPA and Cloud Computing).

Data warehouse and integration systems are set up at large health systems and academic medical centers. They may have established a data warehouse to store information from their EMRs, administrative systems, and employee and patient surveys. This information may be used for medical research, analysis for operational improvements, or evaluation of human resource or training programs [e.g., Northwestern Medicine Enterprise Data Warehouse (NMEDW), http://www.feinberg.northwestern.edu/research/cores/units/edw.html; Research at Trinity Health, http://www.trinity-health.org/body.cfm?id = 695&fr = true].

Automated storage and retrieval may be used in large warehouses run by suppliers and large health systems, such as Intermountain Health. Some smaller versions of these systems might be found in facility storerooms or pharmacies. In hospital units, dispensing cabinets may be considered a form of automated storage and retrieval for pharmaceuticals. Each patient has a separate drawer that is opened by the caregiver through the EMR and contains the medications that have been delivered from the pharmacy. There are also components that are refrigerated for medications that must be kept below a certain temperature (Vecchione, 2017).

Growth technologies

Growth technologies may be used by very large suppliers and health systems for their supply-chain functions. However, many of these are being developed for use by patients directly. This changes the situation from a centralized location for face-to-face interaction between the provider and the patient to one that can take place anywhere. Any supplies or medications must now be available to the patient close to where he/she lives rather than being delivered to the health-care facility.

Mobility capabilities, such as barcode scanning, are used to manage pharmaceuticals, supplies, and lab specimens. The patient wristband also has a barcode so both the patient and medication or supply barcodes can be entered into the EMR when used. Likewise, the lab specimen can be matched with the proper patient when reporting results.

Wearability in the health-care setting refers to watches or other devices that the patient wears to track heart rate and other vital signs related to the individual's health. For example, the Apple Watch has the potential to monitor symptoms of patients and medication responses (Spitzer, June 5, 2018). Apple also has received a patent for a blood-pressure monitor worn by the patient and able to communicate wirelessly with another device (Spitzer, June 8, 2018). These devices can be connected to a central location via the Internet of Things (IoT), and if something is not normal, the provider can be notified. This, along with video conference calls, allows the individuals to "visit" their provider from anywhere and their vital signs can be monitored. This form of telemedicine is becoming much more common. Initial issues with licensing across states and payment for the service are being resolved. It is especially appropriate for individuals who live in rural areas, after a natural disaster, or to follow those with a chronic disease.

Data analytics is made possible by EMRs, administrative systems, and other sources of data that are centralized in the data warehouse mentioned above. If patterns of usage of supplies and medications can be predicted for certain patient populations, then inventories held centrally and in units can be anticipated. Also, the results of patients seen via telemedicine may result in better planning for deliveries to the patients' residences. As in other organizations, predictive analytics can be used to determine when maintenance of equipment may be needed to avoid unplanned events. This is especially important in diagnostic, therapeutic, and surgical areas where a machine breakdown can have fatal results.

Social media is used by health systems to communicate with their patients and as part of their public relations efforts. The supply-chain professionals in the system can also benefit from networking with their counterparts from other organizations.

Emerging technologies

Technologies that have been used in other industries are now being used in some health-care organizations and have the potential to improve the quality of care available to patients, regardless of their location.

Potential applications of *3D printing* in health care are similar to those in manufacturing. There has been much research in the medical areas using 3D Printing. Medical devices and hip and knee joint replacements might be fabricated specifically for a patient when needed and researchers are trying to make organs ultimately for use in patients. Manufacturers are also fabricating spare parts for machines using 3D printers, as needed, rather than having to keep inventory. Who does the fabricating and the impact on the traditional supply chain remains to be seen?

3D Printing in Health Care https://www.youtube.com/watch?v = P2peq82e8is

3D Printed Knee Joint https://www.youtube.com/watch?v = mbyT0sQIM18

Drones for delivery of pharmaceuticals and medical supplies provide service to rural areas and after natural disasters. Amazon has been developing drones for delivery to individual customers. On May 29, 2018 the company earned a patent for various methods of communicating with the customer at the delivery point (Bean, May 30, 2018). A drone was also used to deliver medications to a community clinic in Wise County, Virginia. This is a very rural area where there is no local pharmacy.

Drone Delivery of Pharmaceuticals to Wise County, Virgini https://www.youtube.com/watch?v = iHH4eB__LCMa

Autonomous vehicles have been used in manufacturing, warehouses, and are being developed as passenger vehicles by Tesla, Uber, GM, and others. They are also being used by some health-care systems to deliver supplies throughout a large medical campus. For example, Cleveland Clinic uses them throughout its campus to deliver supplies to various facilities and units.

Cleveland Clinic Automated Delivery Vehicles https://www.youtube.com/watch?v = 1uGTUtqOVnE

Exponential technologies

Blockchain

As described in Chapter 2, Technologies in supply-chain management and logistics, a blockchain is a digital ledger that cannot be altered. "This decentralized, digital ledger system uses algorithms and encrypted keys in linear blocks of time to create a sequential chain that ensures a level of verification and trust" (Landro, 2018). Blockchain is being considered by many but adopted by few. In an SAP survey of 3500 domain experts, 90% view blockchain as an opportunity, but only 3% are actually using it (Bowman, 2018).

In 2013 the Drug Supply Chain Security Act (DSCSA) was enacted by Congress. It "outlines steps to build an electronic, interoperable system to identify and trace certain prescription drugs as they are distributed in the United States" (FDA.gov). These regulations make the blockchain a potential solution for the pharmaceutical supply chain. To address these issues and to develop a prototype solution the MediLedger Project was begun in 2017 by a group of pharmaceutical manufacturers and wholesale distributors. Its 2017 Progress Report is available online and has determined that the approach is feasible.

Pharmaceuticals and other items that are temperature-sensitive also lend themselves to using blockchain and IoT devices to guarantee the temperature remains at the correct level from beginning to the end of the supply chain. An example using SAP's IoT product and IBM's blockchain software shows how blockchain can be used to transport items securely from the manufacturer to the hospital, making sure the temperature stays below the required level is found below.

One challenge is the large amount of computer power required to implement the blockchain solution. The MediLedger project requires 2000 transactions per second versus eight transactions per second currently required (Landro, 2018). Another issue is the difficulty of getting all members of the network to agree to the terms of a transportation contract (Bowman, 2018).

Example of Using Blockchain for Hospital Cold Chain

Identifying Counterfeit Drugs using Blockchain

IoT is part of the wearables described above, which allows patient vital signs to be sent to their provider. It is also used for medical devices such as pacemakers and insulin pumps so that providers can be notified if something is wrong or to change settings remotely. IoT is used in the sensors used to measure temperature during shipping and with RFID in inventory management. The risk of patient harm as a result of breaching the Internet-connected devices is a major consideration as the use of these devices expands.

IoT and Health Care

Virtual reality/Augmented reality is being used for patient treatment and for medical education. Simulations are developed to put the patient into the situation that may cause stress and then a therapist works with them to overcome his/her anxiety. Simulations are also used for medical education to supplement traditional learning strategies (Craig, & Georgieva, August 30, 2017).

Artificial intelligence (AI) used in personal assistants has the potential to recognize symptoms and make suggestions. Of course, Amazon Echo can also be used to order supplies, nonprescription medicines, and medical equipment for delivery to the individual's home.

Future of health care and impact on supply chain

There are many external factors impacting health care in general and traditional health-care organizations. The aging population results in an ever-increasing number of people who are qualified under Medicare for health-care services. The payment structures, amounts paid, and quality data requirements must be met by providers. Mergers among hospitals, outpatient facilities, and physician offices have increased dramatically, reducing the benefits of traditional supply-chain arrangements. Amazon, JP Morgan, and Berkshire Hathaway are also combining forces to form a health-care company led by Atul Gawande, MD, MPH, for their employees to reduce costs and which may have a direct and an indirect impact on the entire industry (Ross, July 9, 2018).

Amazon is moving to disrupt health care by using its existing distribution systems to enter the medical device and supply market in the United States. It has been talking to hospital executives and has tested the Amazon Business services in a large hospital system in the Midwest. Amazon Business is a separate business-to-business marketplace (www.amazonbusiness.com), currently available to support the supply-chain needs of the health-care industry (Paavola, Feb 13, 2018).

Amazon has acquired more than 10 wholesale pharmacy licenses from state pharmaceutical boards that are needed to sell medical equipment to licensed professionals and announced its acquisition of Pillpack in June 2018 (Bresnick, July 5, 2018). A recent survey by Reaction Data found that 62% of the hospital leaders support Amazon as a medical supplier (Paavola, May 15, 2018). With the continued decentralization of health-care services to outpatient facilities and the patient's home, Amazon's infrastructure will potentially meet future needs.

In an article on "The Future of Hospitals," Laura Landro summarizes the basic shift from large, central acute care facilities to many specialized smaller facilities located in multiple locations. Innovative programs, such as the Hospital at Home program run by Mount Sinai Hospital in New York, bring supplies, equipment, and providers to a patient's home rather than having them stay in the hospital. Follow-up services are available for 30 days (Landro, 2018 and mountsanai.org).

Other health-care systems, as well as payers, are focusing on keeping patients healthier, thus avoiding hospitalization. These programs target individuals with chronic diseases, such as diabetes, asthma, and heart failure, as well as working to avoid the onset of chronic conditions. Geisinger Health System serves a number of counties in Pennsylvania where there is a high incidence of Type 2 diabetes. It began working with patients in Shamokin, PA, to provide diabetes education as well as healthy food, cooking equipment, and recipes. There has been a decrease in blood-sugar levels for participating patients (Landro, 2018 and Geisinger.org).

Future potential of technology in the health-care supply chain

The impact of technology in the health-care supply chain is both direct and indirect. Access to providers will no longer be just face to face but utilize telemedicine, mobile devices connected to the Internet, remote tracking of patient conditions, and decentralization of health-care facilities. In order to serve the needs of these patients the supply chain must be able to accommodate delivery of supplies and medications to the patient's location through the use of e-commerce as it exists today as well as drones and automated vehicles in the future.

Increased access may result in more complete data regarding patient conditions in the health-care systems EMRs. When these are combined and analyzed, the resulting clinical, operational, and administrative data may lead to better management of chronic conditions as well as care of acute illnesses. Predictive analytics, machine learning, and AI are all being used in this effort (Bresnick, July 9, 2018). This may lead to better quality outcomes and potential cost savings. It also should result in better inventory management and distribution to health-care facilities and patients.

Traditionally, the percent invested in health-care supply-chain management is lower than that in other industries. As reimbursement levels are reduced by both government and private payers, and a greater number of patients have high deductible insurance and pay for services themselves, there will be an incentive to reduce costs. Applying maturing technologies, such as inventory optimization, sensors, and automated storage and retrieval, may be utilized as well as the recognition of supply chain as a strategic asset.

The high cost of pharmaceuticals and medical devices also provides an incentive to use technology to ensure that items are kept at the appropriate temperature, can be tracked from the point of origin to use in a patient, and can be identified if recalled. Blockchain, sensors, and the IoT all may be used for transporting these items and then scanning their unique identifiers into the patient's record.

3D printing has great potential for manufacturing medical devices for cardiology and surgery. Transportation needs would change to accommodate this new technology. There is also ongoing research to produce organs for transplant using 3D printing which would eliminate the need for human donors and the related transportation to the recipient.

References

Bean, M. (2018, May 30). *How Amazon's latest patent would let customers interact with delivery drones*. https://www.beckershospitalreview.com/supply-chain.

Bowman, R.J. (2018, June 11). Blockchain for the supply chain: Reality vs. hype. *Supply Chain Brain*. Retrieved from http://www.supplychainbrain.com/think-tank/blogs/think-tank/blog/article/blockchain-for-the-supply-chain-reality-vs-hype/.

Bresnick, J. (2018, July 8). *Top 10 disruptive companies to watch in the healthcare space*. https://healthitanalytics.com/news/top-10-disruptive-companies-to-watch-in-the-healthcare-space.

Bresnick, J. (2018, July 9). *54$ of healthcare pros expect widespread AI adoption in 5 years*. https://healthitanalytics.com/news/54-of-healthcare-pros-expect-widespread-ai-adoption-in-5-years?eid = CXTEL000000376574&elqCampaignId = 5760&elqTrackId = 1af9f839ce904ce2acd6157b2bde4eeb&elq = 64c9abdd3b424dc0b5ef88a49d01148d&elqaid = 6167&elqat = 1&elqCampaignId = 5760.

Burns, L. R. (2002). *The health care value chain: producers, purchasers, and providers*. San Francisco, CA: Jossey-Bass.

Craig and Georgieva. *VR and AR: Driving a revolution in medical education and patient care*. https://er.educause.edu/blogs/2017/8/vr-and-ar-driving-a-revolution-in-medical-education-and-patient-care.

Drug Supply Chain Security Act (DSCSA). Retrieved from https://www.fda.gov/Drugs/DrugSafety/DrugIntegrityandSupplyChainSecurity/DrugSupplyChainSecurityAct/default.htm.

Endicott, C. (2017). *When data brings peace of mind: seeing hospital inventory clearly*. Essential Insights on cardinalhealth.com.

Guidance on HIPPA and Cloud Computing. https://www.hhs.gov/hipaa/for-professionals/special-topics/cloud-computing/index.html.

Intermountain Healthcare. https://intermountainhealthcare.org/supply-chain-organization/about-us/.

Landro, L. (2018). *The future of hospitals*. WSJ.com.

Paavola, A. (2018, February). Amazon pushes to become a major hospital supplier: 7 things to know. *Becker's Hospital Review*. Retrieved from https://www.beckershospitalreview.com/supply-chain/amazon-pushes-to-become-a-major-hospital-supplier-7-things-to-know.html.

Paavola, A. (2018, May). 62% of hospital leaders support Amazon as a medical supplier. *Becker's Hospital Review*. Retrieved from https://www.beckershospitalreview.com/supply-chain/62-of-hospital-leaders-support-amazon-as-a-medical-supplier.htm.

Ross, C. (2018, July 9). *As Atul Gawande steps into a risky health CEO role, here are five challenges he faces.* https://www.statnews.com/2018/07/09/atul-gawande-health-ceo-risks/.
Schneller and Smeltzer. (2006). *Strategic management of the health care supply chain.* San Francisco, CA: Jossey-Bass.
Shi and Singh. (2017). *Essentials of the U.S. health care system.* Burlington, MA: Jones & Bartlett Learning.
Spitzer, J. (2018, June 5). *5 Health-related announcements Apple made at its developers conference.* https://www.beckershospitalreview.com/healthcare-information-technology.
Spitzer, J. (2018, June 8). *Apple's latest patent is for a blood pressure monitor.* https://www.beckershospitalreview.com/healthcare-information-technology.
The MediLedger Project. (2017) Progress report. Retrieved from https://uploads-ssl.webflow.com/59f37d05831e85000160b9b4/5aaadbf85eb6cd21e9f0a73b_MediLedger%202017%20Progress%20Report.pdf.
Vecchione, A. (2017, January) Dispensing cabinets provide greater capacity/touch screen. *Drug Topics*. Retrieved from http://www.DrugTopics.com.
Wolper, L. E. (2011). *Health care administration: managing organized delivery systems* (pp. 573–605). Sudbury, MA: Jones and Bartlett Publishers (Chapter 15, Sheyer and Fridman, Material and Resource Management.

Further reading

Geisinger Fresh Food Farmacy. https://www.geisinger.org/freshfoodfarmacy.
Gupta, M. (2017). *Block chain for dummies (IBM Limited Edition).* Hoboken, NJ: John Wiley & Sons, Inc.
Hospital at Home (HaH) and Observation Unit at Home (ObsaH) – How it Works. https://www.mountsinai.org/patient-care.
Where Blockchain Meets Cold Chain. (2017). *Wall Street Journal.* Retrieved from http://partners.wsj.com/ups/blockchain-meets-cold-chain.

CHAPTER 7

The emergence of new containers in cold chain

Sang Moon
Department of Business Administration, Hankyong National University, Anseong, South Korea

Contents

Introduction

Changes in cold-chain environments

The international transport of temperature-sensitive products is an essential link between producers and consumers. Over the past years, the characteristics of the retail food industry that usually requires a cold-chain environment have been transformed by worldwide trade. The development of infrastructure, facilities, equipment, and technology across the cold chain, the faster lead time of transport, and the liberalization of the global economy have driven consumers' demands for year-round availability of fresh fruit and vegetables. Maintaining freshness requires a more efficient supply chain, including the transportation and storage of highly perishable agricultural products. Maintaining freshness is the most important factor in international trade.

Technology in Supply Chain Management and Logistics
DOI: https://doi.org/10.1016/B978-0-12-815956-9.00007-7

The trade-off between responsiveness and cost of a product's transportation is clear in the agricultural product trades. To reduce transportation costs, most countries are exporting agricultural products, including fruit, fish, flower bulbs, and meat, via sea transport. Sometimes transit times of the products may be longer than the shelf life. Consumers demand year-round supplies of agricultural products without considering seasonality. However, the relatively short shelf life of agricultural products may increase inventory carrying costs because of spoilage.

Perishable products, including agricultural products, food, and pharmaceutical products, should be transported under temperature-controlled conditions to lower the temperature to extend their storage life. Perishable products may be divided into frozen and chilled cargo. Maintaining freshness of fruit and vegetables in international trade requires chilled conditions using various transport equipment across the supply chain.

The proper temperature-controlled environments of agricultural products may extend their shelf life and freshness compared to products that are not under the proper environment. This is mainly because agricultural products "breathe." When the products are shipped above the proper temperature, the products accelerate "breathing" and lose freshness. In other words, nonproper temperature-controlled environments decrease agricultural products' shelf life and cargo quality in the international supply chain.

The proper temperature-controlled environment starts with the post-harvest processing of agricultural products because the respiration of the products is usually higher at room temperature than at low temperature. Therefore many producers, carriers, and retailers try to transport and store agricultural products at as low a temperature as possible. However, excessively low temperature is not the answer to maintaining freshness since it may result in a physiological change known as "chilling injury." Tropical and subtropical agricultural products, such as bananas, melons, avocados, mangoes, and papayas, are known for "chilling injury" risk. Therefore the proper temperature for agricultural products is the most important factor throughout the entire supply chain. However, the proper temperature to maximize shelf life is specific to each product.

According to Dynamar (2015), fresh produce that requires a temperature-controlled environment accounted for 2.7% of world trade via ocean transport in 2015. It is estimated to have reached about 105 million tons in 2015 and expected to grow further. It is predicted to expand by 4%–5% annually. Increases in the world population and average incomes may stimulate seaborne trade of fresh produce. Ocean transportation is still the major transportation mode in agricultural trade because most agricultural products are relatively heavy and bulky, and less valuable.

The dominant products that are transported globally in temperature-controlled environments are the agricultural products, including bananas, which are the single most important reefer (refrigerated) cargo. Meat, fish and seafood, dairy products, flowers, and pharmaceuticals also require temperature-controlled environments.

Challenges to shippers

Reefer shipping via ocean transportation plays an important role in cold chains across the globe. It is facing the challenge of surprisingly dynamic, complicated, and fragmented logistics. The critical requirement of temperature-sensitive cargoes is to deliver the products in the same condition/quality as they were shipped. Main reasons for damage to temperature-sensitive cargo carried in reefer container ships are poor stowage by the shipper, lack of vessel/container preparation for handling, such as lack of general cleanliness, off-power or off-refrigeration of vessel/container, incorrect temperature settings, failure to monitor temperature, and poorly precooled or overcooled cargo.

As temperature-sensitive products deteriorate at a rate that is temperature dependent, temperature maintenance is the most critical issue. Frozen products require the maintenance of low enough temperatures to prohibit deterioration effectively. Chilled products must be maintained at the lowest possible temperature that may not reduce the quality of the product.

There is no technology available to stop the process of agricultural product maturation. The only possible technology is to slow the process. When a product is already too mature to sell during transit time, a buyer may reject it and file a damage claim, even though a carrier provides reasonable care and handling. To avoid this problem the entire transit time of agricultural products from growers to consumers must never get too close to the overall shelf life.

For agricultural products, temperature control, humidity levels, proper packing, and air ventilation become extremely important to extend shelf life and maintain quality. Because the characteristics and requirements of agricultural products vary from commodity to commodity, handling processes and temperature-controlled environments may vary as well. Some products, such as meat, have to be kept chilled between 0°C and −2°C or frozen at colder than −18°C. Other products, such as fresh fruit and vegetables, have to be kept chilled between −3°C and +16°C to ensure the best possible quality.

The trend of the last few years has been the reefer container taking over from the specialized reefer ship. More than half of all specialized reefer ships have been scrapped, and there is a dramatic decline in the orders of specialized reefer ships. The share of specialist reefer ships in international trade had decreased from 60% in 2000 to an estimated 26% in 2014 (Dynamar, 2015). Today, reefer containers are more widely used to transport temperature-sensitive products than specialized reefer ships since specialized reefer ships can only transport bulky products and are inflexible. As the volume of refrigerated product increases, a shift from the use of dry containers has become clear. The use of reefer containers has many advantages, such as the possibility to transport relatively small volumes and being able to access many liner connections using container ships.

In many cases, agricultural products that are low value are transported by dry container for cost reduction even though these are temperature sensitive. The freshness declines, the damage of goods frequently occurs, and the global competitiveness of fresh logistics is low. Products (igniters, EPS resins, etc.) that ignite at high temperature must be transported using a container that can be temperature maintained, but accidents can happen. For example, in the case of the equatorial passing route, the inside temperature of the container is approaching 80°C during the transportation, and the cargo ship could potentially burn due to the explosion set off by internal ignition. This happened in 1986 with the Hyundai Merchant Marine and 2011 with a Maersk ship.

Advanced postharvest technologies and cold-chain technology are essential to reduce food waste and to maintain high standards of safety and quality. Controlled atmosphere (CA) and modified atmosphere packaging (MAP) may be alternative technologies for decreasing agricultural products' metabolic activity and increasing shelf life. Also high-insulated containers may be another alternative. Both CA and MAP technologies and high-insulated container technology have been applied to change the cold-chain paradigm and have benefitted from technological innovation.

Concepts for new containers

Controlled atmosphere container

Atmospheric gases naturally consist of about 79% nitrogen, 20.9% oxygen, and 0.03% carbon dioxide, with the remainder compromised of noble gases.

Agricultural products under cold-chain environment may still be respiring during transporting and storing activities with natural atmospheric gases while the cold-chain environment may extend the shelf life of these products. Cold-chain environment with refrigeration may slow down degeneration in the quality of the agricultural products. However, yeast, mold, and aerobic bacteria may grow in a cold-chain environment. Also in an enclosed environment, the composition of atmospheric gases may be rapidly changed due to the respiration of the agricultural product. Therefore a simple cold-chain system is not sufficient to extend the shelf life of agricultural products that are respiring.

Advanced postharvest technologies, such as CA and MAP, are essential for extending the shelf life and maintaining quality. CA and MAP with refrigeration make the degeneration in quality slower in the cold-chain system. CA and MAP are technologies in which the atmospheric gases around agricultural products are different from natural atmospheric gases. CA is a technology for substantially changing an atmosphere with respect to the concentrations of CO_2 and O_2 levels. Since the mixture of the atmospheric gases keeps changing because of metabolizing and ripening of the agricultural products, the atmosphere needs to be constantly monitored and adjusted for predetermined CO_2 and O_2 levels.

MAP is a relatively passive technology compared to CA. MAP is airtight packaging that prohibits the flow of atmospheric gases. In an airtight environment, agricultural products will keep respiring until O_2 gas is gone since O_2 is required for the respiration. Since O_2 gas is reduced, the respiration rate of the products can be slowed too. The same effect occurs when CO_2 gas is increased. In addition, high concentrations of CO_2 may prohibit the growth of yeast, mold, and aerobic bacteria.

Both CA and MAP decrease O_2 levels and increase CO_2 levels since both of these activities slow respiration and ripening of agricultural products. CA and MAP are usually used to change or control the composition of air inside a cold-chain environment. With an increase in shelf life, CA and MAP may slow the metabolic rate of agricultural products resulting in securing and preserving their eating quality, such as the firmness, texture, appearance, and crispness of the products. The optimum condition of agricultural products in terms of O_2 and CO_2 levels may differ for each product. It means that the optimum CA condition may vary considerably from one product to another.

The CA container has been developed to minimize spoilage and to increase the shelf life of agricultural products during transportation.

Since MAP is packaging technology, only CA technology is applied to containers. A CA container is a reefer container with CA technology. CA containers control the composition of the atmosphere inside the container. This may have the same effect as the CA storage for enhancing shelf life. Since agricultural products are usually transported by ocean transportation in international trade, the relatively long transit time of ocean transportation may negatively influence the shelf life and quality of the products. Therefore the use of a CA container is a dramatic game changer to extend the shelf life and maintain the initial quality of agricultural products at the origin throughout a shipment's entire journey.

High-insulated container

An insulated container is used to maintain a certain temperature for the products inside. The insulated container is very similar to a cooler that is used by individuals. The insulated container prevents any exchange of outside air and transfer of outside temperature through the body of the container. In other words the insulated container should not be affected by external factors. All products in the container should be safe and secure from the external environment, especially heat. The insulated container does not require a power supply to control temperature. This is the main reason that the insulated container is distinguished from a reefer container that controls the temperature inside.

Insulated containers are usually used to transport temperature-sensitive products a short distance. Since the insulated containers do not require a power supply, these can be used for any transportation mode that can handle the container itself. It can also be stored in any place without a power supply. Reefer containers periodically require special care for handling because there is a generator outside of the container. Thus special care is needed to avoid damage to the generator during the handling process. However, insulated containers do not require this kind of special handling. Moreover, reefer containers are about 10 times more expensive than dry containers. The freight rate of reefer containers is about three times higher than those of dry containers. High prices and high freight rates result in increased logistics costs.

Insulated containers usually use urethane foam of more than 20 cm depth in every section to insulate the container. Utilizing urethane foam has several disadvantages, such as decreasing the inside volume of the container and inconvenience of handling cargo. Adding 20 cm urethane foam in every section of the container reduces the container capacity. In particular, adding urethane foam on the floor increases the height of the container floor, which may make accessibility of a forklift difficult and further reduce the capacity of the insulated container.

A high-insulated container can use other material, such as fumed silica, to reduce the disadvantages of using urethane foam since fumed silica is thinner than 3 cm. The insulation property of fumed silica is eight times higher than urethane foam. Fumed silica is usually used for high-end refrigerators, high-class building materials, and transporting small containers/boxes with outstanding insulation properties but high costs.

Phase change materials (PCMs) for thermal energy storage are another alternative to urethane foam as an advanced energy technology. "PCM is a substance with a high heat of fusion which, melting and solidifying at a certain temperature, is capable of storing and releasing large amounts of energy. Heat is absorbed or released when the material changes from solid to liquid and vice versa; thus, PCMs are classified as latent heat storage (LHS) units" (Wikipedia). PCMs can absorb thermal energy above a predetermined temperature level or release it below predetermined temperature levels during the phase transition process. PCMs may be able to be utilized in a high-insulated container as insulation since PCMs are widely used in the cold-chain system. However, PCMs are known for low thermal energy storage and leakage during the phase transition process.

Impacts of new containers on cold chain

Present status of container technologies

Controlled atmosphere container

Many ocean shippers are interested in developing CA containers as well as container manufactures. Maersk Container Industry (MCI), a subsidiary of Maersk, developed a CA container called Star Cool CA system. Star Cool CA system is built into the Star Cool integrated reefer container, which is already utilized in international trade. Star Cool CA monitors and controls the amount of O_2 and CO_2 inside the reefer container. It has been shown that Star Cool CA can extend transportation windows of bananas and avocados as much as 45 days. Star Cool CA was developed to reduce energy consumption by reducing the overall weight of containers up to 100 kg while it adds CA equipment into the reefer container. MCI launched Star Cool CA + system, which is an extension of the Star Cool system. Star Cool CA + is used for low-respiring products, such as blueberries and lychees, since these low-respiring products require a different composition of the atmosphere inside the container. Star Cool CA + can be transferable to all Star Cool CA containers so that Star Cool CA + provides a wider range of cargo types under CA conditions. Since the Star Cool CA(+) system monitors the environment and condition of cargo as well as controls, the system provides information about any problem if it occurs.

APL launched the SMARTcare + system for products requiring a CA. SMARTcare + may increase the postharvest life of some agricultural products up to three times compared to other conventional methods. SMARTcare + also alleviates physiological disorders during transportation, including chilling injury, and extends longer voyage periods and distances by maintaining freshness and quality of the products. SMARTcare + may handle fresh fruit and vegetables, including apples, asparagus, avocados, blueberries, broccoli, cherries, grapes, papayas, mangoes, nectarines, peaches, and plums.

Hapag-Lloyd introduced the ExtraFresh and Everfresh systems. These systems are very similar to other companies' systems. The Hapag-Lloyd CA system may extend transportation windows up to 35 days for avocados, up to 45 days for bananas, up to 28 days for blueberries, and up to 28 days for mangos. Hapag-Lloyd adopted several CA technologies, such as Thermo King's automatic air freshening system, Everfresh system, E-autofresh, and Maxtend. The system can be applied to any products with proper CA technology, upon request.

The CA technologies have evolved with the development of more precise and dynamic control systems, called dynamic CA (DCA). DCA is applied to storage activity since CA was originally developed for storage. The purpose of DCA is to minimize possible oxygen levels and to change the composition of gases in the container in response to physiological changes of products inside. DCA is very attractive because it can control the atmosphere inside the container in near real-time with existing CA technology. DCA may extend storage life longer than existing CA technology.

High-insulated container

There are several container manufacturers building insulated containers. Those manufacturers usually use urethane foam for insulation. There are several disadvantages to using this foam. The Korea Railroad Research Institute (KRRI) developed a high-insulated container with fumed silica to overcome the disadvantages of urethane foam. KRRI developed the container originally for the Korea Polar Research Institute (KPRI) in the Antarctic. Utilizing fumed silica for an insulated container is their very first attempt. KPRI needed to store the experimental equipment during the winter season in the Antarctic. Since it is extremely cold during the winter season, most experimental equipment failed after the season when it was stored in a conventional container. KPRI requested that KRRI develop an all-new container that can maintain thermal energy during winter season since the reefer container requires a power supply and the conventional insulated container does not maintain proper conditions inside the container. KRRI shipped the high-insulated container to the Antarctic in the fall of 2017.

The high-insulated container developed by KRRI may also be used for transportation and storage of products needing temperature management. Since the safety of drugs and food have become important issues, drugs and food needing temperature management are shipped usually by a reefer container to extend the shelf life and ensure quality. However, the relatively higher freight rates of the reefer container are a factor increasing the price of the products in importing countries. Thus the high-insulated container may be utilized for shipping products needing temperature management at a lower cost than reefer containers (Fig. 7.1).

As a result of KRRI's environmental laboratory experiments, it was found that the target temperature (20°C–0°C) holding time inside the high-insulated container was about 9 hours when the outside temperature was −30°C, about 2.25 times longer than the 4 hours of the reefer container without a power supply. The internal temperature of the dry container shows almost the same behavior as the change in the outside temperature. When the outside temperature is 60°C, the retention time of the target temperature (20°C–0°C) in the high-insulated container shows almost the same performance as the abovementioned low-temperature test (Fig. 7.2).

As mentioned, KRRI uses fumed silica for insulation material that was developed by OCI, which is one of the leading chemical companies in Korea. Fumed silica is more expensive than urethane foam but has a greater insulation property. However, adding fumed silica to a container is more difficult than adding urethane foam since fumed silica has a definite form and is very weak on impact. Because of the definite form of fumed silica, several panels are needed to cover one side, and there should be a gap between panels. The floor of a container covered by fumed silica

Figure 7.1 The high-insulated container developed by KRRI. *KRRI*, Korea Railroad Research Institute.

Figure 7.2 Inside of the high-insulated container.

should withstand weight and impacts caused by access of a forklift since a forklift is usually used to handle cargo in the container. Therefore OCI developed a special method of construction to bridge the gap and to endure impacts on the container.

The fumed silica may be used in a reefer container and a CA container, which is needed to enhance insulation properties. Since urethane foam is still used for reefer and CA containers, the fumed silica may be a good substitute. This may increase insulation properties, but with increased construction costs.

The high-insulated container has another advantage compared to a reefer container. The transportable volume of a reefer container is relatively small compared to that of a conventional container. However, the transportable volume of the high-insulated container is almost the same as a conventional container. Thus when there is no cold-chain cargo for the high-insulated container, it can be used as a conventional container since a similar volume can be provided with no power supply.

Case studies of the effects of the new containers on the cold chain

With these CA containers, exports of fruits and vegetables in the Asian region by Japan are increasing dramatically, led by Japanese shipping company NYK Line. According to the Ministry of Agriculture, Forestry, and Fisheries in Japan, the export value of Japanese agricultural and forestry products recorded the highest ever amount of 236.8 billion yen (about 2.1 billion US dollars). The increase in the export of agricultural and marine products from Japan has been due to the use of vessels with CA container technology.

Sales started with a Hong Kong supermarket chain and began exporting using the NYK Line vessel in 2016. The company ships agricultural and marine products from Hakata Port in Kyushu Fukuoka to Hong Kong once a week by the CA container. Hong Kong's supermarkets provide a place for about 30 items of Japanese agricultural and marine products with a sign saying "Direct Kyushu Market." The number of supermarkets in Hong Kong, which sell the products, has increased to 16. "Kyushu Agriculture and Fishery Products Direct" plans to extend its "Direct Kyushu Market" to Singapore.

The freight rate of ocean transportation with CA container is reduced to one-tenth of that of air transportation from Fukuoka to Hong Kong. NYK uses CA containers developed by Japan Daikin Industries, the world's largest air conditioning equipment maker. The amount of Japan's agricultural and marine products that are price competitive by reducing freight rates are rapidly increasing in the Hong Kong market with the use of CA containers. In Latin America, where there are many exports of agricultural products, there is a growing preference for the CA container rather than the conventional reefer container. Demands for CA container technology is increasing since 700 containers among 5500 containers that NYK ordered in 2015 were CA containers.

Growth potential for controlled atmosphere containers

New containers may increase ocean freight transportation demands in two ways. One is the "substitution effect," and the other is "creation effect." The substitution effect results in demand for new containers by those who currently transport freight by reefer or dry containers. Shippers prefer lower freight costs for goods requiring temperature control. In the case of certain agricultural products the quality of which moderately declines, despite concerns about the deterioration in quality, dry containers have been used. However, as new containers emerge, cargo that used dry containers, even though it requires temperature control, is expected to result in increased quality of the cargo in the market. The "substitution effect" is expected to be mainly represented by relatively inexpensive cargo at short distances. For example, various Korean vegetables and fruits are exported to Japan using the shortest ocean route because of concerns about the deterioration in quality by extended transport time. However, the high-insulated container may be used in transport without the concerns of deterioration of the cargo. This cargo can be transported directly to the major consuming market in Japan by ocean transportation. This means that it is possible to minimize the utilization of road transportation to reduce transportation costs from ports to a consuming market since road transportation is more expensive than ocean transportation. However, the freshness of cargo can be maintained.

Creation effect is an effect of new containers on freight demand by those who transport freight by ocean transportation instead of air transportation because of relatively lower freight rates. Shippers prefer shorter transportation times for goods requiring temperature control. In the case of certain agricultural products the quality of which sharply declines, despite the high shipping cost, air transportation has been used. However, as new containers emerge, cargo that used air transportation will be using ocean transportation, which is expected to increase price competitiveness of the cargo in the market. The "creation effect" is also expected to be mainly represented by relatively inexpensive cargo at short distances.

For example, all natural matsutake mushrooms in Korea are exported to Japan using air transportation. By using CA containers that can control the temperature and humidity as well as the atmospheric gas, it is possible to utilize ocean transportation to maintain nearly similar freshness, but at cheaper freight costs to domestic consumption areas in Japan.

The high-insulated container can be used as a transport container for cold-chain transportation in the general logistics market. It can be utilized as a medium supplement between the reefer container with high logistics costs and the dry container that has no insulation performance in the transportation of cold-chain products. Cold-chain transportation is soaring in Asia, such as in China, Japan, Thailand, Vietnam, and Korea. It is unnecessary to have a power supply and is used for railway transportation of temperature-sensitive cargo, such as fresh food and dangerous goods. Especially, Trans-Siberian Railway, which has recently increased its trade volume, is used as a means to prevent cargo damage due to low temperature when passing through cold winter area.

Conclusion

With the development of transportation and logistics systems, consumers expect the year-round availability of fresh agricultural products while the products are not even produced in the country. Unlike the past, a market for agricultural products has been expanded. In other words, it is not necessary to distinguish agricultural products into domestic and import. Therefore qualities, such as freshness, firmness, appearance, texture, and crispness, of agricultural products are selling points in the market as well as costs. Maintaining quality has become a critical point in agricultural trade. It requires more efficient transportation and storage activities.

The CA container applies CA storage technology that controls the atmosphere, such as O_2 and CO_3, in the sealed container. CA technology can extend the shelf life and maintain the quality of agricultural products so that a market for the products can be extended. Similarly, the high-insulated container maintains the quality of the products as the temperature in the container is maintained without a power supply. Both containers provide essentially the same function to maintain the quality of the products. However, one is best for long transportation times, and the other is best for short transportation times.

Increasing demand has led to the development and the introduction of new container technologies, such as CA and high-insulated containers.

The new containers can be a game changer in the cold-chain industry and agricultural trade. Consumers, retailers, producers, and shippers want to have more reliable transportation methods for agricultural products to extend shelf life and to maintain quality since transport time is usually the longest part of the entire supply chain.

The development of the new containers may stimulate agricultural trade since these enhance the entire supply chain value including maintaining the quality of the products and lowering freight expenses. It is believed that current shipments by air transportation may be able to shift to the new containers because of lower freight rates. Conversely, the new containers may create a new demand for international transportation of products that are not traded previously because of various reasons, such as volume, weight, and price.

Changes in consumption trends are also affecting the transportation sector. The more diverse consumer demands, the more diverse transportation demand will be expected. In terms of agricultural trade, however, relatively long and expensive transportation has always been a problem. The new containers are expected to help meet the various consumer demands and to solve this problem, even though the technologies are not breakthroughs. It is believed that newer technologies in cold-chain system will emerge soon. However, in the short run, the new containers will enhance social welfare in the world.

Reference

Dynamar. (2015). DYNAMAR Reefer Analysis: Market Structure, Conventional, Containers.

Further reading

CMA CGM homepage. (April 2018). https://www.cma-cgm.com/.

Falagan, N., & Terry, L. A. (2018). Recent advances in controlled and modified atmosphere of fresh produce. *Johnson Matthey Technology Review*, *62*(1), 101–117.

Hapag-Lloyd homepage. (April 2018). https://www.hapag-lloyd.com/.

International Cold Chain Technology. (2011). Controlled Atmosphere and Modified Atmosphere Guidelines Refrigerated Cargo Ships and Refrigerated Containers.

Kim, J., & Moon, S. (2014). The competitive effects of low cost carriers in Korea: Focusing on Jeju Route. *Journal of Shipping and Logistics*, *30*(1), 275–295.

Korea Polar Research Institute homepage. (March 2018). http://www.kopri.re.kr/.

Korea Railroad Research Institute homepage. (March 2018). http://www.krri.re.kr/html/kr/.

Huang, L., & Piontek, U. (2017). Improving performance of cold-chain insulated container with phase change material: An experimental investigation. *Applied Science*, 7.

Maersk Container Industry homepage. (April 2018). https://www.mcicontainers.com/.
NYK Line homepage. (April 2018). https://www.nykline.com/ecom/CUP_HOM_3000.do?redir = Y.
OCI homepage. (March 2018). http://www.oci.co.kr/.
Samad Bodbodak and Mohammad Moshfeghifar. (2016). *Advances in controlled atmosphere storage of fruits and vegetables* (pp. 39–76). Research Gate.
Wikipedia. (August 2, 2018). https://en.wikipedia.org/wiki/Phase-change_material.

CHAPTER 8

Unlocking digital innovation: guiding principles for driving digital technology in the supply chain

Matthew Liotine
Department of Information & Decision Sciences, University of Illinois at Chicago, Chicago, IL, United States

Contents

Introduction

Companies are faced with the problem of how to leverage what they have and how they can drive further benefits through digital innovation. Today's businesses are facing the forces of change, driving them to make decisions to digitally innovate their business models and operational processes. In today's environment, companies are shifting from a "run-the-business" attitude to a "change-the-business" mentality. Innovation is now critical to any business and should be encompassed not only as a business strategy but also as a business process. Thinking big goes beyond just making a new product or technical development—it is the creation

Technology in Supply Chain Management and Logistics
DOI: https://doi.org/10.1016/B978-0-12-815956-9.00008-9

of new means of bringing value to the firm. While companies play with methodologies to innovate their business models, innovating engrained business processes can be even more challenging. Companies have turned to technology to help innovate their business processes, but it requires using a decision methodology that can assure relevant outcomes.

Typically, all kinds of digital technologies continuously appear on the horizon that entice firms into embracing within their operating environments. The early adopters are those that exploit the "first-mover" advantage by taking the lead to use such technologies to transform their business models and processes. Leading edge companies ultimately dominate markets and enjoy high returns by codifying knowledge for data-driven decision-making. These enterprises are known for continuously developing technology strategies since they do not want to fall prey to the famous Alvin Toffler quote "if you don't have a strategy, you're part of someone else's strategy." Successfully adapting a technology requires an understanding of the relationships between risk and the opportunity it brings.

Supply chains are turning toward digital strategies in order to manage the growing complexity that is arising from demand patterns that are becoming increasingly dispersed and diverse. Simply put, a digital supply chain is one that utilizes data and systems to connect operations and business functions internally and externally with trading partners and relevant stakeholders. By intelligently connecting these processes, businesses can achieve greater managerial visibility of their operations and improve decision-making with the end-goal of improving growth and profitability. New technologies, such as the Internet of Things, artificial intelligence, machine learning, blockchain, quantum computing, and many others, can create new opportunities for supply chains to make radical changes in their operating models. However, the challenge for many companies is to craft business and innovation strategies that can reduce the risks of investing in digital technologies. In this chapter, we review conventional methods of enacting supply chain digital innovation, and how they are being replaced with newer rapid and cost-effective innovation methods.

The digital supply chain

Research suggests that digital supply chains can increase annual earnings by 3.2% and revenue growth by 2.3% (Gezgin, Huang, Samal, & Silva, 2017). At the very least, digital technologies help reduce supply chain complexity by recording transactions and consolidating data. While enterprise resource planning systems have been in use for some time, these systems are primarily systems of record, maintaining databases that contain master and transaction data tables. However, digital innovation goes beyond employing technologies solely within systems of record. Employing digital technology to develop systems of intelligence can provide insights, solve problems, and help make decisions that would not be otherwise achievable by manually distilling information from enterprise systems of record. Systems of intelligence can connect and combine cross-functional data from diverse sources, and analyze it to identify, or even anticipate operational problems. Such technology can make traditionally inexact tasks, such as demand forecasting and capacity planning, more precise (Gezgin et al., 2017).

Much of this thinking is reflective in the current worldwide fourth industrial revolution, also known as the Industry 4.0 movement. This is an initiative to seamlessly integrate supply chains with continuously available smart factories (Harris Williams & Co., 2017; Price Waterhouse Coopers, 2016). It focuses on the end-to-end digitization of production assets and integrating these with supply chain partners, while analyzing and seamlessly transferring data between them. Driving this movement are the strides in factory automation, which have taken place over the last several years, now coupled with the trends in digitalization of value chains and product and service offerings, business models, and customer access. Consequently, the rapid onslaught of technologies arising from this movement, some of which are disruptive, has created a more complex and dynamic ecosystem for growth and innovation (Pagani, 2013a, 2013b), since digital strategies can connect diverse firms through various channels.

Supply chain networks, which are traditionally vertically and linearly integrated, are shifting to more horizontal forms through peer-to-peer connectivity. Furthermore, the friction of information between physical and digital assets is being reduced through integrated technologies and cloud-based digital platforms that can facilitate and simplify information exchanges among supply chain entities. These characteristics are helping companies transform historically linear single-sided business models into networked, multisided models, such as the freemium and long-tail models. To adapt to these changing conditions, firms must continuously, incrementally, or radically innovate their supply chain processes in order to stay relevant and profitable. This is easier said than done since digital innovation can be capital intensive and involves risk-taking on the part of the enterprise.

Risk-averse innovation requires acquiring knowledge throughout the entire innovation process so that well-informed decisions can be made along the way. The use of modeling, simulation, virtualization, digital twins, and other techniques can be effective decision-analysis tools. However, cognitive innovation also requires an understanding of the maturity levels and business processes across the supply chain ecosystem, which may not always be at comparable levels. Companies that are high performing innovators typically leverage their ecosystems through communal innovation and partnerships.

What is innovation

By definition, innovation is the introduction of something new, either a new idea, method, or device. In the field of supply chain management, it is changing the way supply chains do things. Technology is often viewed as a critical mechanism to innovate since it is how companies transform labor, capital, materials, and information into goods and services. Quite often, innovation is associated with the development of new products or services, or through the adoption of new technology. But technology is not necessarily the only way to enact change. The mechanisms of change can vary and take on different forms, which can be used in various combinations:

- A *technical* innovation, such as introducing a platform, feature, service, interoperability, system, application, component, or data
- An *operational* innovation, such as introducing a process, method, model, procedure, formula, recipe, or material
- A *human* innovation, such as introducing new skills, people, roles, and responsibilities
- A *monetary* innovation, such as introducing new capital or financing
- A *managerial* innovation, such as introducing new organization, governance, administration, or oversight

What qualifies a change as an innovation from the conventional view depends on the degree to which the changes and improvements are carried out. Fig. 8.1 illustrates the following distinctions between improvement levels (Government of Western Australia, Department of Primary Industries, & Regional Development, 2017):

- *Continuous* improvements are typically in the form of progressive upgrades to sustain process and product optimization over time, which are characteristic of most firms.

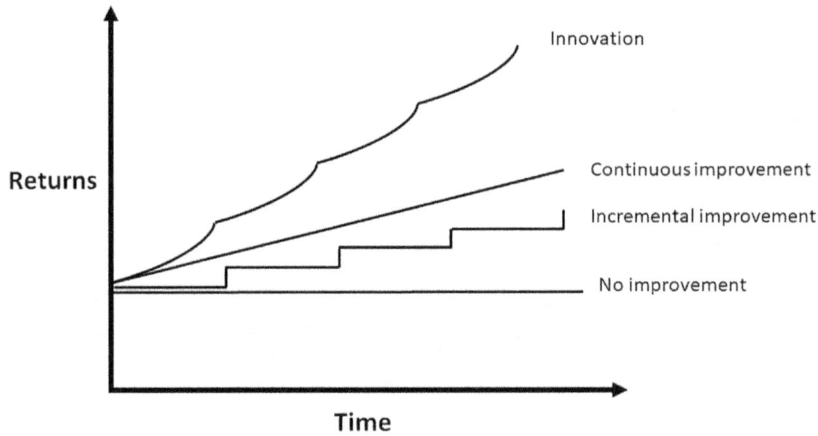

Figure 8.1 Distinction between improvement levels.

- *Incremental* improvements are typically discontinuous in the form of process upgrades, product line extensions, internal cost savings, productivity gains, and so on.
- *Innovation* improvements use radical, disruptive approaches to completely transform how a process is executed, typically through the use of technologies, products, operations, or business models.

The methods used to plan and appraise these kinds of improvements can be quite distinct from those used in planning continuous or incremental improvements.

Digital innovation involves leveraging technology or using information to create capabilities that can improve processes to the degree where they can be transformed. The mix of process improvement and new capability forms an innovation frontier (Fig. 8.2). The mix of technology and process upgrades can drive improvements from merely being progressive to becoming truly radical in nature. So, for example, using existing technology to transform a process can be just as innovative as introducing a new technology to the firm in order to enhance an existing process.

Disruptive innovation deals with the pace of technology adaption within a firm's core products or processes. Historically, technologies often progress faster than demand, surpassing the needs of their market at the time of their introduction. The pace of their price–performance characteristics often exceeds the performance improvement that is required or

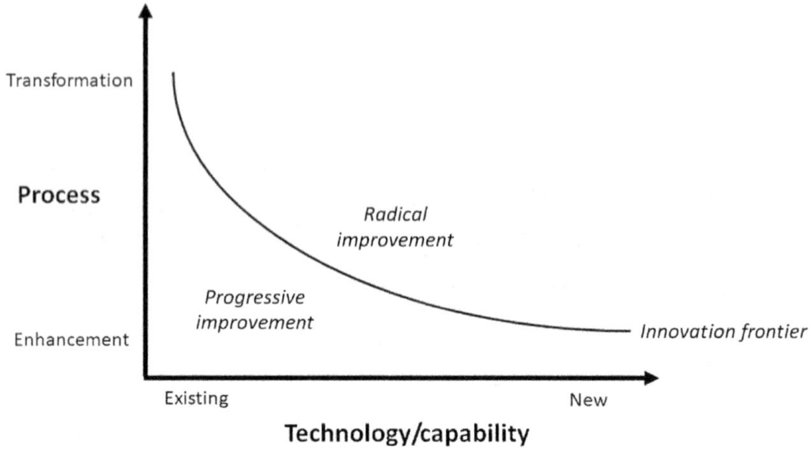

Figure 8.2 The innovation frontier.

can be absorbed by the market. Disruptive technologies are typically born in acute markets or applications, serving a very specific need, versus the mass markets. Mass markets are typically broad, homogeneous, and stable in nature and are quite often very product driven. Acute markets, sometimes referred as "precision markets," can focus on a very specific product, process, or customer base. In either case, product or process innovation is crucial to create added value, which is the contribution to the product's utility to end users (Pagani, 2013a, 2013b). The definition of value can be vague at times and can change as customer needs evolve. From a production standpoint, value constitutes those features that improve the product for the customer, particularly those aspects that the customer cares about. Concentrating solely on eliminating nonvalue-added activities, a concept promoted in Lean Six Sigma practices, may not solely constitute an innovative improvement. These kinds of innovations involve achieving lower costs by reducing inventory and increasing both utilization and throughput, assuming low demand variability.

But customers convey their value statement at the time of product purchase and may not necessarily care about how a company produces the product. Thus effectively improving value-added activities, whether a customer knows about them or not, needs careful consideration. For example, improving customer response by increasing inventory and decreasing utilization in order to drive higher sales are strategies that are opposite to those used in eliminating nonvalue activities (Pound, Bell, & Spearman, 2014).

Barriers to innovation

When companies fail or lose market share, it is mainly due to ignorance of some basic innovation principles. Digital innovation involves using technology to transform labor, capital, materials, and information into goods and services. While digital innovation can result in declined performance at the outset, the costs per unit of performance gradually decrease as the market use of technology becomes more widespread. Products or processes based on disruptive technology are usually cheaper, simpler, smaller, and easier to use or execute. History has shown that while companies do a fairly good job at continual process improvements related to their core, mass-market products, and services, they either overlook or are unable to justify innovations that are born out of acute markets. Eventually, the price performance of these innovations declines to the point where their mass market appeal overtakes that of a firm's legacy products, reducing their market share and disrupting their business. Fig. 8.3 illustrates this concept, which is sometimes referred to as the "innovator's dilemma" (Christensen, 2016).

In addition to overlooking innovation potential, companies that try to innovate quite often fail in the execution of the overall innovation process. This includes the following:

- *Failing to identify ripe areas* for innovation within their firm. Companies that seek growth in dynamic or mature markets soon discover that there are many segments that are not growing rapidly.
- *Employing a lengthy and costly innovation process* versus promptly developing ideas, involving rapid prototyping methodologies.

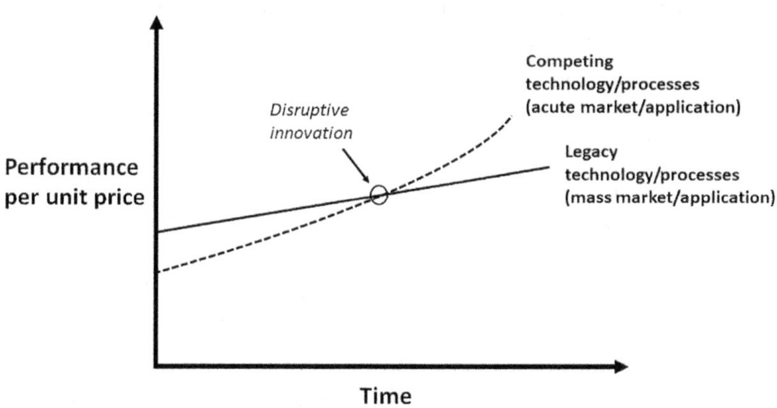

Figure 8.3 Disruptive innovation.

- *Limiting ideas to those generated solely within their own firm* versus seeking ideas and knowledge beyond the boundaries of their company.
- *Not recognizing the required modes of improvement* that a technology can enable, such as streamlining activities, expanding capabilities, and enhancing processes or products.
- *Tailing-off of initial innovation* of products or processes and reverting to original levels due to lack of support.

Many of these pitfalls in enacting innovation within the enterprise are a result of a variety of factors that are characteristic of large companies. In companies where lines of business managers dictate product or process upgrades, improvements tend to be unleashed on a project basis versus an ongoing process or program basis. While this is not necessarily an undesirable feature, it opens up the possibility of project thrashing in response to competing business priorities. Companies will err on the side of creating many low-risk short-term incremental improvement projects instead of driving toward the few that might entail higher risks but with greater rewards. In addition, it can result in a "set it and forget it mindset," in which further improvements are not explored beyond the completion of a project. Embedded legacy processes and ingrained cultures can also add to the innovation friction, creating artificial constraints and limited views toward change. Limiting the innovation responsibility to only the firm's research and development (R&D) organization, which is inherently expensive, can slacken progress without reducing innovation costs. It can also foster a "not-invented-here" mentality, which is counter to today's conventional wisdom that promotes a more open and communal approach toward innovation.

Another barrier to innovation is the difficulty in creating a viable business case for a product or process improvement. Companies that listen to their customers and identify new products or capabilities promising greater profitability and growth are rarely able to build a business case for investing in them. Those with a return on investment (ROI) focus will have a difficult time appraising an innovation using the same scorecard that is used for mainstream processes or products. Using the same criteria to appraise high-margin mainstream products cannot accord priority to innovations that might initially provide low margins at best. Appraising innovation requires shifting the mindset from ROI to growth. If an innovation is to be appraised, the appraisal must be based on the potential of the innovation relative to the acute market or application for which it is defined versus its performance relative to an already embedded base of products or processes. The ultimate goal of a business case is to outline the risks associated with a prospective investment so that management can decide on an appropriate course of action. Risk is a four-letter word, which many companies dislike. It conveys what a firm is willing to gamble and translates into a fear of the unknown or of incapability (i.e., making a mistake). History has shown over and over again that inaction itself can be a mistake and even be fatal. Thus the recipe for a viable business case is to define the unknowns up front and develop an innovation plan that can harness the powers of the prevailing organizational forces to change course based on learned outcomes.

Innovation philosophy

The criteria used in making and prioritizing decisions typically reflect the values of an organization. While many companies recognize that innovation is critical to business growth, they fall short with respect to execution. After all, a successful innovation must concurrently solve a business or customer problem and generate returns, which is not an easy task. The first and most challenging step in defining such a solution is identifying the need that dictates the goals and reasons for the innovation. Identifying a need involves identifying what a process or customer is trying to accomplish without predetermining a solution. This is why sometimes trying to satisfy explicit or stated customer needs can lead to false solutions. Henry Ford once said, "If I had asked people what they wanted, they would have said faster horses." Instead, looking for implied needs, which are not stated nor obvious but can yet lend insight into the rationale of what a process or a customer is trying to achieve, can remove limiting assumptions that can predispose certain types of solutions. Establishing the customer's point of view requires empathy, that is, placing oneself in the shoes of the customer.

Common approaches to innovation reflect an organization's underlying philosophy toward change and risk appetite. *Zero-based* philosophies are those that involve starting from scratch and seeking entirely new approaches to products or processes. These are usually the game or sea changing technologies—products or services that can have widespread effects on business and society. Companies, such as Amazon, Tesla, Netflix, Apple, and others, are known for this kind of innovation. These approaches typically employ funnel-based methods, which are discussed further in this chapter. These methods can be expensive and entail higher risks while producing successes that are few and far between.

Opposite to this philosophy is *microphilosophies*. These are more incremental and focus on resolving a specific pressing need. This involves fixing what is broken and pivoting on to the next problem. This could involve developing new ways of transforming activity into productivity by reinventing suboptimal processes or substituting current methods with new ones. While this reflects a more risk-averse approach, it can be prone to the pitfalls of employing the strictly project-based innovation approach that was mentioned earlier. Furthermore, it can create change fatigue within a supply chain, which results when trying to make too many changes at once.

Regardless of what philosophy is involved, digital innovation within a supply change constitutes using information to make radical improvements in understanding and affecting the key factors that govern the supply of goods: variability, capacity, and cycle time (Pound et al., 2014). Demand variability can drastically increase cycle time, which is the time required to produce a product. Thus the ability to use digital technology to sense demand and to communicate variability to production processes could enable them to adjust capacity to achieve acceptable utilization levels without increasing cycle time or inventory, which is typically in the range of 70%–80%. Fig. 8.4 illustrates the relationship between variability, utilization, and cycle time. The area between the current and desired levels represents the opportunity that digital innovation could deliver to a supply chain process.

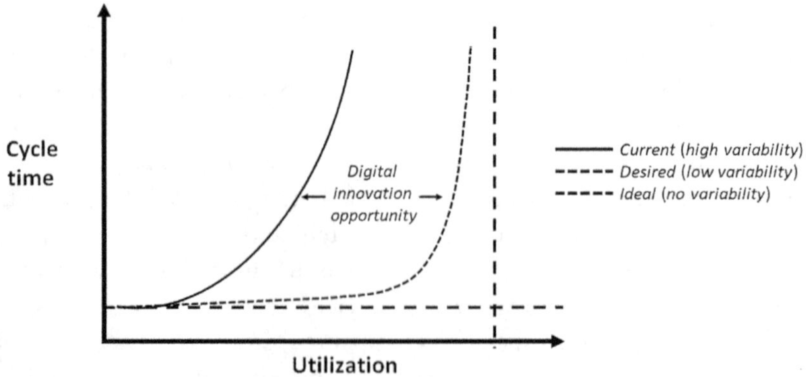

Figure 8.4 Supply chain digital innovation opportunity.

Innovation techniques

There are two general classes of innovation techniques: inorganic and organic. Inorganic techniques confine the responsibility of innovation discovery to mainly within the company. The company relies, to a large extent, on its R&D resources or product development departments to seed and incubate new process improvements or product ideas. Occasionally, companies might purchase innovations from other firms as well. Nevertheless, the firm bears most of the risks and costs since the effort and decision-making are confined to within the company. This class of techniques typically employs funnel methods, which historically are costly and yield low success rates.

Organic techniques are those that leverage the ecosystem of the firm. With the help of outside disruptors, such as external business partners, suppliers, vendors, startups, or universities, different organizations can collaborate on ideating new products and processes. Unlike inorganic methods, these techniques spread risks and costs across collaborators and have proven to be more successful. Firms engaged in collaborative knowledge sharing, either internally within the company or externally with other companies, exhibit stronger innovation performance. While there are risks of knowledge leakage, these risks can be moderate and do not offset the potential innovation benefits (Ritala, Olander, Michailova, & Husted, 2015).

Furthermore, given the global nature of today's supply chain processes, it is also shown that internal collaboration with offshore business units or external companies does not necessarily improve innovation performance (Frenz & Ietto-Gilles, 2009). Thus firms do not need to look far for innovation partners.

Effective innovation methods have one thing in common: a plan for learning what needs to be known. The most frequent unknowns are those about the customer of the product or process: the definition of value from their perspective, the customer's stated and/or implied needs, how they view and measure process performance, how they would like the process to perform, and how they think the process can be improved. While the customer might not be the appropriate source to define an innovative solution, per Henry Ford's famous quote, finding answers to these questions can lend insight into the possible range of feasible and viable solutions.

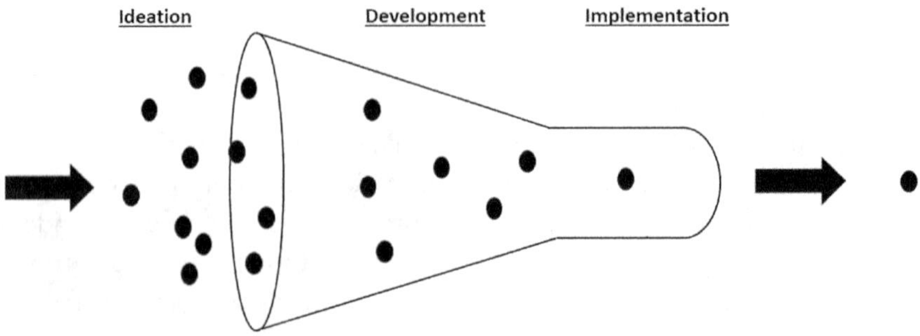

Figure 8.5 The innovation funnel.

Funnel methods

Innovation funnels are popular and have been used for quite some time. While there are many variants of this method, it boils down to a few major steps: start with many ideas, narrow them down to a shortlist using specified criteria, and then select the one or two to progress to the implementation stage. Fig. 8.5 illustrates this approach. Such methods are often used for product innovation versus process innovation. While nearly all big-branded businesses employ this approach, 8 out of 10 brand extensions fail (Nichols, 2007). In addition to the low success rate, there are numerous other reasons why funnels tend to be ineffective. These include the fact that the trial and error process can be long and expensive, since many ideas are later discarded, ultimately wasting the development costs to vet them. Furthermore, given the fact that this approach involves a competition among ideas confined to a selected set, creativity could be stifled by overlooking other worthwhile possibilities that lie beyond. More importantly, the mission of this contest-like approach is to pick a winner, and not necessarily *create* a winner. The funnel is also an underlying model for business and technology accelerator incubators, which are organizations that are sponsored by outside firms to breed and harvest new business ventures. The performance and success rate of such organizations have been known to be less than stellar (Butz, 2015; Relan, 2012). Yet, funnel methods can be useful for certain kinds of new product initiatives and still continue to be used. The method can also be used as an ideation tool to screen an initial list of ideas prior to further vetting.

Rocket methods

Innovation rockets are nearly the reverse of innovation funnels (Nichols, 2007). These methods employ a collaborative ideation process with the

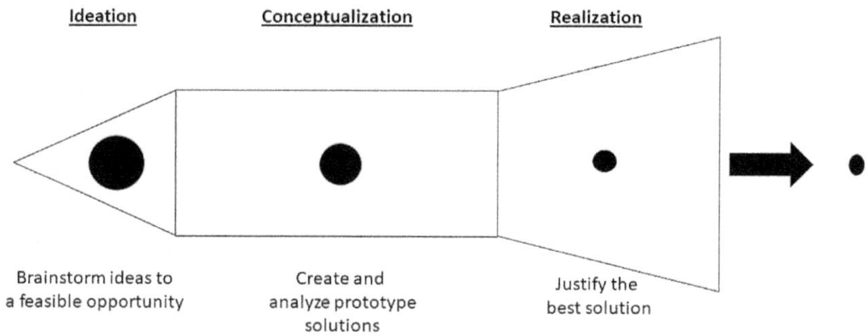

Figure 8.6 The innovation rocket.

end-goal of stimulating a particular change or achieving a goal. They use a template of inquiry to go from the abstract to the concrete—to brainstorm concepts that get to the essence of understanding the potential of an innovation from different viewpoints and translate them into high-level executable project action plans with estimated time frames. The process entails a comprehensive imagineering of the opportunity to produce a compelling strategy for innovation and reduces uncertainty by vetting impactful issues up front to avoid unintended consequences. It evaluates and filters the major pieces of unstructured information and lends some structure to the overall effort. It blends elements of problem seeking, design thinking, Six Sigma, Quality Function Deployment, business process transformation, and project planning into a framework that is rapidly implemented, saving time and costs. The approach is best executed in an environment supported by a creative, collaborative, and diverse cross-functional team of participants who can provide inputs from across the firm to anticipate and circumvent potential obstacles and preestablish buy-in from the participating organizations. These methods also help crystallize an understanding of the innovation strategy and use the results to communicate it to others. The method is illustrated in Fig. 8.6.

Ideation phase

This first phase of the method, also referred to as the define phase, brainstorms opportunities to find the right thing to do. Its purpose is to define a specific problem of the customer or process. It requires digging into the customers' stated or implied needs, as previously discussed. Sometimes the process is conducted using a conceptual map in the form of a predefined canvas to frame out the basis for the innovation, as illustrated in Fig. 8.7,

Figure 8.7 An innovation canvas.

much in the same way canvases are used for business model generation (Osterwalder & Pigneur, 2010). The canvas serves as a lens through which users can initiate the analysis from any perspective, much in the same way an artist creates a painting—in an organic fashion wherever the brush takes them versus a sequential manner.

The canvas is partitioned into "perspectives," each of which represents a particular dimension of the decision. The following describes each perspective:

- *Segment*

  The segment perspective represents the particular scope within the enterprise that is being served. It can be in terms of a customer or niche market, a product or product group, service or business unit, a business function, or whatever classification identifies who would benefit from the innovation. It could even represent a new or unreached market segment. Its purpose is to develop boundaries and limits for the improvement, with the intent of identifying the start and end points of the segment and processes that are the focus of the analysis. The segment will convey the level(s) of authority that may be required to complete the innovation, the cost limitations of the innovation, and the party responsible for financing. It also defines the area of influence of the innovation.

- *Opportunity*

  The opportunity perspective could be the most challenging to render. It conveys the need, reason, or impetus for the improvement or benefit being sought. One might think of it as a problem statement, but it may not necessarily be born out of prevailing pain points, but out of insight or awareness. Identifying the opportunity requires a comprehensive review of current conditions and capabilities. Sometimes this requires asking situational questions that include facts about the current situation that can help reveal where problems exist. This also might require the ability to imagine things that might not currently exist or to view the current process from the customer's perspective. Opportunities will typically arise in several situations:

- A crisis with an existing process
- Modifying an existing process to adapt to a changing environment
- Introducing a new product or service offering
- Preparing for the future by testing out a new concept

Problems should convey a difficulty or dissatisfaction with the current situation, which could imply certain needs. The effects or implications of each problem could drive the type of pay-off needed to resolve the problem and lead to alternative types of explicit outcomes that might be desired.

- *Reward*

  The reward space conveys the value proposition. It serves as an informal business case of the benefit of the improvement that is being sought. The reward can be stated either quantitatively and/or qualitatively and should focus both on the near and long term.

- *Technique*

  This perspective describes how the innovation will deliver its value. It describes what techniques will be used to drive the corrective actions that will effectuate the rewards or value, in other words, those things the innovation would need to provide in order to exploit the opportunity. It conveys the method for improving functionality that will be imparted by the innovation.

- *Team*

  The team perspective is rendered with the stakeholders who will be affected by the effort. This includes those who will be participating in planning and executing the initiative, both internal and external, such as buyers, suppliers, and customers. The initiative should have a champion who can convey progress to upper management.

- *Process*

  The process perspective outlines the operational process(s) that will be either modified, replaced, or newly created by the digital innovation. Supply chain processes comprise how an organization creates, delivers, and captures value for a particular good or service. These processes must evolve with business models, social trends, and new enabling technologies. For each process a simple diagram is created showing the process inputs and outputs with regard to information and/or materials, the customers receiving the outputs, and the sources of the inputs. The steps of the process should be outlined as well. Tools that can be used in conjunction with this analysis include system–input–process–output–customer, turtle, value stream, or time-phased diagrams.

- *Risk*

  The risk perspective is included in order to integrate the risks with the opportunity to reveal the potential threats and consequences associated with implementing the innovation. It should reflect the overall risk attitude of the firm and its willingness to go ahead with the implementation, considering this risk.
- *Resources*

  The perspective defines the enablers to enact an effective implementation toward achieving the desired outcome. This includes resources in terms of people, money, equipment, systems, infrastructure, and technology.
- *Horizon*

  This perspective defines the time frame for capitalizing on the opportunity and achieving the rewards.

The perspectives do not have to be completed in any particular sequence but can be completed in several iterations, if desired, sometimes referred to as sprints. For each sprint the following are defined for each perspective:

- Goals and objectives sprint

  Goals indicate what the firm wants to achieve and why. "Lip-service" or "general motherhood goals" are avoided. Goals can be driven by needs—a requirement for an essential state, thing, or quality. When citing goals or outcomes, evidentiary information should be used to the extent possible to authenticate the need. While using any factual information to back up assertions is helpful, it is important to note that the focus of the exercise is beyond fact finding. Ultimately, the statements used to render this part of the canvas should convey what need is being addressed and what outcome is desired to satisfy the need. For each goal, several objectives are identified. Objectives are more specific than goals—they are things that need to be achieved to obtain each desired outcome. They need not convey how the outcome is to be achieved.

- Milestones sprint

  Several milestones are defined for each objective. Milestones are, traditionally, events that mark the accomplishments to carry out the completion of an objective.
- Tactics sprint

  For each milestone, tactics are identified. These are actions or tasks that must be completed to reach the desired milestone. Each action should convey how the outcome is to be achieved. The tactics across all perspectives are later used as the basis for high-level project plans that can be detailed in later phases. Creating project plans provides a level of assurance that the innovation can be implemented.

The method requires using a beginner's mindset that could involve asking naïve questions and dealing with ambiguity and uncertainty until concepts are converged upon. Successful ideation first results in numerous ideas without the worry of them being either bad or good. The feasibility of each idea is then assessed within the canvas, inherently vetting ideas as they are generated.

It is important to perform these sprints as a group exercise. A live interactive session is typically the best and easiest way to carry out the approach. Using visual tools, such as a whiteboard, sticky notes, or flipcharts, can portray and organize ideas to provide visual thinking and to communicate and understand concepts. All goals, objectives, and milestones are numbered, and their relationships among each other are maintained throughout the analysis. Not all perspectives need to be completed or "rendered" fully before going to the next phase, and the entire process can be iterated as often as needed.

Depending on the nature of the firm and needs, the methodology can be executed in several ways. Some firms may already have a handle on the desired opportunities they would like to explore. For other firms the process may have to be preceded with a session that assesses numerous opportunities and then reduces these to a shortlist of the most imperative ones for further analysis. Several canvases can be created, either for the same or different innovations. In addition, a canvas could also be created for both the present and future states if needed.

Conceptualization phase

The purpose of this phase is to frame the reality of the innovation further by testing it out in some way to gain assurance that the right thing is being done or to understand what conditions need to be in place to make it work. This phase develops an operational model or prototype as a thinking tool to analyze the performance and economic merits of a single or alternate solution to reduce the number of alternatives to a shortlist. The analysis would involve creating some kind of digital duplicate, using common best practice approaches, such as simulation, optimization, value stream analysis, crossover analysis, and other modeling methods. The model and analysis are typically delivered via a spreadsheet, but other software tools might be used as well. This phase uses the prototype to evaluate different modes of operation or delivery of the product or process within the future or ideal state. The purpose is to identify the potential cost and benefits to be used as input to appraising the business case to justify the potential innovation.

Realization phase

This perspective defines how the success of the best alternative will be appraised by the stakeholders, including the champion of the effort or upper management. It conveys the critical success factors—the criteria and standards by which the innovation's success will be judged. This requires an understanding of the improvements delivered by the innovation within the future or ideal state relative to the current state. The states should comprise specific requirements that the solution should include, which are operationally defined and measurable, and mutually agreed upon by stakeholders. Meaningful metrics must be devised and assessed relative to a baseline state versus on an absolute basis. Furthermore, the appraisal should include qualitative assessment as well.

Excessive detailed measuring of the innovation could discourage radical improvement (Richtner et al., 2017). Using ROI as the sole basis of decision-making inherently assumes what the completed innovation could return, in the absence of a realistic idea of its real worth. As an accounting metric, ROI is used to compare revenues with investment expenses. In accounting, standard cost models are designed to allocate revenues to expenses for financial statements, allocating fixed costs over the volume of units produced, implying that producing more units will lead to lower unit costs. For this reason, these costs may not be applicable to the kind of operational models developed in the conceptualize phase. Instead, fixed costs should reflect the up-front investments in the innovation. Annual recurring costs should also be stated, whether they are either fixed or variable (Pound et al., 2014). Another caveat with using ROI for appraising an innovation is that it compares the innovation to the status quo of products or processes as a basis for comparison, a pitfall cited earlier. This thinking ultimately encourages short-term incremental improvements versus long-term breakthrough ideas (Morris, 2017).

It should be noted that while both the rocket and funnel methods are displayed as sequential processes, there, in fact, is an opportunity for feedback loops between phases, if needed, depending on how they are executed. In addition, the two methods need not be mutually exclusive and could be conducted in parallel or nested within each other. For example, prospective solutions within an innovation funnel can each be vetted using an innovation rocket approach.

Appraising innovation efforts

Developing a balanced scorecard is often the most effective means of appraising digital innovation efforts. Such scorecards should be developed at the portfolio, process, and project levels (Slone, Dittmann, & Mentzer, 2010). At the heart of innovation, appraisal is the concept of economic profit, sometimes known as economic value added, which is defined as net income less the cost of capital. Net income, or net operating profit after taxes, will improve with innovations that reduce costs and increase sales. Innovation efforts must, therefore, affect these two variables in order to show some merit. Higher sales with lower invested capital will increase margins and cash flow. Higher sales can be achieved by generating revenue using digital technology to improve customer order fill rates and reduce stockouts to increase product availability. Achieving these with less inventory and increased cost productivity will also improve cash flow. Consequently, increased customer satisfaction can reduce customer churn and generate new customers. Less inventory will reduce working capital, increase capital turnover, and ultimately improve ROI since total capital will be reduced.

The following list summarizes some key quantitative and qualitative attributes that can be used in assessing innovation according to three categories (Anthony, 2013):

- *ROI* metrics that characterize the financial value of the innovation portfolio based on investments and returns, with awareness of the previous mentioned caveats. These metrics could be forward-looking, measuring expected outcomes, or backward-looking, reflecting historical outcomes, of the current portfolio. They can be used to view and coordinate net profit management over all initiatives:

    - Profitability (net income over sales)
    - Operating efficiency (sales over assets)
    - Financial leverage (assets over equity)
    - Return on equity (net income divided by equity) that is the product of the previous three metrics
    - Return on equity divided by successful projects
    - Actual versus targeted breakeven time
- *Organizational capability* metrics that characterize the firm's success rate in executing high-level profit innovation initiatives:
    - Number of patents filed in the past year
    - Royalty and licensing income from patents/intellectual property
    - Number of new products, services, and category businesses created
    - Percentage of sales from products introduced in the past X year(s)
    - Successful innovation projects divided by total projects invested
    - Percentage of revenue or profit from products or services introduced
- *Leadership* metrics that characterize the organization's innovation efficiency, reflective of a culture that fosters growth, open innovation, and granular grassroots initiatives:
    - Annual R&D budget as a percentage of annual sales
    - Percentage of capital invested in innovation projects
    - Total R&D headcount or budget as a percentage of sales
    - Number of active projects
    - Number of projects divided by total capital and operational investment
    - Number of ideas submitted by employees
    - Number of projects conducted with external entities
    - Percentage of employees undergoing innovation training
    - Number of formal innovation processes

Appraising innovation effectiveness and efficiency requires the ability of a company to track activity (e.g., projects, processes, and tasks) and financials. The former may be more challenging than the latter to track and may require the use of business process management and/or project management systems to record data that can be joined with financial information. More importantly, project designations for innovation projects that are not necessarily tied to profit centers need to be defined. In addition, indicators that can capture successful project outcomes should be devised. One method is to create a list of criteria designating whether an innovation project can be viewed as successful upon completion.

The goal of digital innovation is to effectuate supply chain improvement. The following are the most typical goals of supply chain improvement attributed to digital innovation:

- *Increased operating income margin*, with the intent of reducing costs with greater operating leverage, can be achieved through the following objectives:
  - Reduced cost of goods sold as a percent of revenue through reductions in transportation costs, warehouse and inventory management costs, efficient supply chain network design, reduced procurement costs, and improved outsourcing;
  - Reduced selling, general, and administrative costs as a percent of revenue through reductions in customer service, supply chain administration, and information technology costs;
  - Increase in revenues, even from within mainstream customers or markets, and reducing customer price sensitivity;
  - Reduce depreciation and amortization as a percent of revenue.
- *Increased capital utilization* with the goals of improved cash flow and better management of working capital through reduced cash operating cycle times, which increases asset velocity. Working capital comprises inventory, accounts receivable, and net accounts payable. This can be achieved through the following objectives:
  - Reducing days in inventory through improved transportation, warehouse, and inventory management, and efficient supply chain network design. Using digital systems to enlarge inventory visibility can improve demand accuracy and planning.
  - Reducing days of sales outstanding through greater shipment integrity, higher fill rates, improved delivery confirmations, more accurate invoicing, and improved communications with customers.
  - Increasing days of outstanding purchases through improved payment terms and processes.
- *Increased fixed asset utilization*, with the intent of making assets more productive and eliminating nonearning or unneeded assets through increased transport efficiency, improved warehouse management, higher capacity utilization, increased availability, selective outsourcing, and information technology management.

Innovation roadmap

A well-designed and flexible innovation roadmap should make innovation planning easier and ultimately reduce innovation risks by learning what needs to be known. Creating an effective roadmap begins with a vision of how management sees the company unfolding in the next several years. Per this vision, the company must establish its mission statement and then develop supporting goals, strategies, and tactics for its supply chain to achieve the overall mission. Strategies and tactics should ultimately lead to projects. Comparisons between the future and current state will point to process and technology gaps that need to be closed through innovation improvements. An ongoing innovation program consisting of a revolving collection of projects should be formulated to expedite the overall innovation effort.

Unfortunately, there are no best practices for developing innovative strategies. Early decision-making can help vet uncertainty up front, reducing the risk of implementation. The uncertainties associated with planning innovation projects are better handled with flexibility rather than a rigid net-present-value approach. As new findings are discovered, strategies might have to change to avoid adversity. This flexibility can be enacted by defining smaller stepwise projects to reflect various stages of the effort, with the options to defer, expand, contract, or abandon the effort entirely at each phase.

Firms are often reluctant to kick off projects having varying degrees of uncertainty. Conventional investment analysis is frequently used to prove in projects having positive returns that exceed certain rate of return thresholds. Uncertainty is modeled by increasing the discount rate, which can ultimately reduce the desire for undertaking a project. This approach overlooks the possibility that assumptions and conditions will likely change over the course of a project. Adding to this uncertainty is the risk that, while in execution, conditions might change that could render tasks up to that point as wasteful. For this very reason, each project should employ a common innovation process that incorporates the techniques and methods that were discussed earlier in this chapter.

Innovation culture

As was earlier stated, the values of an organization are those criteria that will be used to make, prioritize, and execute innovation decisions. Leading companies that are known for innovation embed an innovation mindset within their culture (Christensen, 2016), which begs the question of the kind of culture required for effective innovation. A culture for successful innovation is one that fosters the freedom to comfortably convey and express ideas, ultimately building a creative confidence within the enterprise. It removes the vertical and horizontal boundaries for cultivating and sharing ideas across the organization. This is why innovation is difficult to achieve in large companies. Such companies will resort to setting up some form of autonomous organization, either internally or externally, with the mission of developing an innovation. Moving the innovation away from the mainstream corporate environment frees the effort of the cultural forces and cost structures that can inhibit progress. Many technology accelerators, incubators, and venture companies are created for this very reason.

Upper management is usually the worst place to look for new solutions—most will likely come from operational, floor, or field personnel. However, upper management can reinforce an innovation culture by enabling innovators to bypass barriers that often stifle creativity and defining the organizational scope and boundaries of innovation (Ishak, 2017). Management can also set clear financial and operational priorities and reserve the resources necessary for expediting the innovation roadmap (de Jong, Marston, & Roth, 2015). Keeping the innovation program moored to the firm's missions and strategies provides grounds for sustaining the required resources and capabilities (Sull, 2015).

Creative confidence in a corporation dispels the myths and attitudes toward what constitutes a good idea. Innovation does not need to involve new technology and can simply focus on significant process improvement or working smarter. Ideas do not necessarily have to be original, such that reinventing the wheel or building a better mousetrap can very well be acceptable (after all, McDonald's did not invent the hamburger). While quite often businesses require that innovations must satisfy a recognizable customer problem, many successful innovations were indeed solutions in search of a problem, such as sticky notes. An innovation mindset should not be fearful of technology or procedural barriers that can obstruct immediate realization. If it is impractical to realize the innovation in the short term, preparations can be made for the longer term. Such active waiting is quite popular in industry, as many companies will wait until a competitor introduces an innovative product to avoid the risks of being a first-mover.

Conclusions

If used effectively, the approaches described in this chapter can be used to vet high-value innovations versus low-value ones relative to the supply chain, product, or customer segments. They can provide the firm with a clear idea of what must be done to make the proposed innovation work and produce an aggressive-but-realistic high-level roadmap for decision-making with estimated time frames. Such methods can rapidly unify and harmonize a strategy across many stakeholders. Outcomes can be shared with team members, the champion and stakeholders to achieve consensus, which merely provides points of departure that could evolve into something new during their exploration. These methods can thus be used as a formidable tool to create a company-wide understanding of opportunities and to sell ideas either internally or externally. This approach is far more likely to connect with stakeholders versus traditional business case methods.

An innovation roadmap should in no way be cast in stone and should be updated regularly as needed. Since customer footprints are constantly evolving, so too must innovation. Firms focusing on ongoing continual improvements view innovation strategy as a process, not a project, and typically enjoy higher returns. Even if outcomes are unusable for strategic or operational reasons, the knowledge obtained may still be of high value. Successful digital innovation projects typically feature improvements that are evaluated rigorously, with prototyping, proof of concepts, and field trials embedded in the rollout to minimize risk. The scope should cover the services, processes, and system requirements for the innovation and should include decision points where changes can be specified. The beauty of innovation is collaborating and sharing ideas that will create things to help others. In order for a firm to be successful, it must make others successful.

References

Anthony, S. (March 2013). *How to really measure a company's innovation prowess*. Harvard Business Review.

Butz, V. (2015). Why startup incubators don't work. *The Next Web*, 18 May.

Christensen, C. M. (2016). *The innovator's dilemma*. Boston: Harvard Business Review Press.

de Jong, M., Marston, N., & Roth, E. (2015). *The eight essentials of innovation*. McKinsey Quarterly.

Frenz, M., & Ietto-Gilles, G. (2009). *The impact on innovation performance of different sources of knowledge: Evidence from the UK community innovation survey* (Vol. 38, pp. 1125–1135). Research Policy.

Gezgin, E., Huang, X., Samal, P., & Silva, I. (2017). *Digital transformation: Raising supply-chain performance to new levels*. S.l: McKinsey & Company.

Government of Western Australia, Department of Primary Industries and Regional Development. (2017). *Improvement tools: Continuous improvement and innovation.* [Online] Available at: https://www.agric.wa.gov.au/improvement-tools-continuous-improvement-and-innovation.

Harris Williams & Co. (2017). *Automation market: HW&Co. Whitepaper.* S.l: Harris Williams & Co.

Ishak, W. (September 2017). *Creating an innovation culture.* McKinsey Quarterly.

Morris, L. (2017). Chapter 6: Innovation Metrics. In: *The Innovation Master Plan: The CEO's Guide to Innovation.* s.l.:s.n., pp. 187–210.

Nichols, D. (2007). *Why innovation funnels don't work and why rockets do.* Autumn: Market Leader.

Osterwalder, A., & Pigneur, Y. (2010). *Business midel generation.* Hoboken: John Wiley & Sons.

Pagani, M. (2013a). Digital business strategy and value creation: Framing the dynamic cycle of control points. *MIS Quarterly, 37*(2), 617–632.

Pagani, M. (2013b). Digital business strategy and value creation: Framing the dynamic cycle of control points. *MIS Quarterly, 37*(2), 618.

Pound, E. S., Bell, J. H., & Spearman, M. L. (2014). *Factory physics for managers.* New York: McGraw Hill.

Price Waterhouse Coopers. (2016). *Industry 4.0: Building the digital enterprise.* S.l: Price Waterhouse Coopers.

Relan, P. (2012). *90% of incubators and accelerators will fail and that's just fine for America and the world.* Techcrunch.com.

Richtner, A., et al. (2017). Creating better innovation measurement practices. *MIT Sloan Management Review, 59*(1), 47–55.

Ritala, P., Olander, H., Michailova, S., & Husted, K. (2015). Knowledge sharing, knowledge leaking and relative innovation performance: An empirical study. *Technovation, 35,* 22–31.

Slone, R., Dittmann, J. P., & Mentzer, J. T. (2010). *The new supply chain agenda: The 5 steps that drive real value.* Boston: Harvard Business School Publishing Corporation.

Sull, D. (May 2015). *The simple rules of disciplined innovation.* McKinsey Quarterly.

CHAPTER 9

Case studies of supply chain technology implementation

Anthony M. Pagano[1], Matthew Liotine[2] and William Stillman[3]
[1]Center for Supply Chain Management and Logistics, University of Illinois at Chicago, Chicago, IL, United States
[2]Department of Information & Decision Sciences, University of Illinois at Chicago, Chicago, IL, United States
[3]Executive Vice President and Co-owner of GAINSystems (retired)

Contents

Technology in Supply Chain Management and Logistics
DOI: https://doi.org/10.1016/B978-0-12-815956-9.00009-0

Introduction

This chapter comprises a series of case studies of specific companies that used and integrated one or more of the technologies, identified in the previous chapters, into their supply chain and logistics operations. This was accomplished by interviewing a select sample of firms to identify the type of technology they have implemented, the problems involved in implementation, necessary user training, and how this new technology interfaced with technology currently in use in the business, among other issues. The chapter describes the results of the interviews.

The first part of the chapter discusses five different companies that implemented several of the technologies discussed in earlier chapters in this book. The companies asked not to be identified. The last part of the chapter discusses three companies that implemented inventory optimization software and the results, including impacts on cost savings, operations, and inventory management.

Company 1 results

Key technologies

This company is currently looking into technologies, such as autonomous vehicles, analytics, business intelligence, and data collection (for most of these descriptive purposes, nothing predictive as of yet), to increase its productivity in the warehouse by providing business insight. It recently implemented a Tier 1 Transport Management System satisfactorily.

In terms of autonomous vehicles the company has put autonomous forklifts to use, but it is currently looking at smarter vehicles, such as the new Fetch Robotics product, which follows a warehouse employee carrying a pallet that can be filled with heavy products. Part of the installation process would be to map the floor plan of the warehouse in the system, so the product can "see" and maneuver its way through the warehouse. It found this to result in lower equipment costs in contrast to a forklift while facilitating improved productivity. There was also a perceived improvement in quality. These were the areas where definite returns were observed.

With regard to implementation, the time to put these products in a company-wide operational environment was estimated to be approximately 2 years. For a single warehouse implementation, this period reduces to 6 months. One of the major changes observed through this process was that the amount of integration needed with the existing warehouse management system has been reduced, with some products not having to interface with the warehouse management system (WMS) at all. The Fetch Robotics solution was chosen to make the environment most suitable to employees while increasing productivity. Another advantage of the particular solution was the price, with a general estimate in tens of thousands of dollars, as opposed to millions of dollars for a standard automated storage and retrieval system (ASRS) system. The solution was also attractive due to its flexibility. With a warehouse that caters to multiple customers, often from different industries, especially with short-term contracts of 3–5 years, it is difficult to estimate a standard requirement and not feasible to install an expensive system that is not as flexible. "The world is more excited about activity systems than storage systems."

Other technologies

The company is also interested in the following technologies:

- Analytics—For reporting purposes
- Voice pick—Implemented at one warehouse, voice pick was found to be easy to integrate, accurate, and improve productivity

Company 2 results

Data warehousing

Data warehousing, in addition to analytics, is one of the more mature technologies in this company. It is constantly working to improve infrastructure and the amount of data captured on this front. Data warehousing is adopted companywide (as opposed to a few business units) and supports automated reporting with business objects. It also has some analytically oriented teams that are more deeply engaged in using R, Python, and SQL to meet ad hoc requirements. This is done in conjunction with third-party software. It also has smaller centers of analytic excellence within various business units, based on requirements.

Access to the data warehouse is regulated by a governance team. Certain teams, based on requirements and expertise, have unrestricted access, while the majority of teams interact with it in the form of dashboards or automated reporting.

GPS

A portion of the 30,000 containers owned by the company has been undergoing GPS unit installation in the past 2 years. These units involve long-living battery-powered sensors that turn themselves on and off on predetermined intervals and also by sensing (e.g., when the doors open). The sensors help improve visibility into the status of the container (full or empty), serving to drive up utilization. In addition, this allows for the provision of location information to customers, and also security assurance. Instead of manual entry of information about the location of the container (often delayed and inaccurate), the sensors allow for an automated entry that is accurate to a few feet.

There are multiple layers of cost takeout involved with GPS. Through improved visibility, there is a direct impact on utilization. Also, due to better utilization, the demand for leasing containers is decreased, adding a second layer of economic value from installing GPS. Drivers can also be deployed more effectively using real-time location information, and loads could be matched more accurately.

Optimization software

The company utilizes software for various layers of optimization, both for long-term planning, in terms of how to optimize fleet positioning, and short-term tactical planning. Other elements of optimization include price optimization. It is currently 18 months postimplementation of PrOS software, a cloud-based price optimization software customized according to industry and the company's own requirements. The company uses proprietary software, developed in-house with the help of consultation, and off-the-shelf software.

Other technologies

The company is also interested in
- mobility and
- cloud computing.

Company 3 results

Optimization software

This company uses an optimization software produced by iLog, an international software company purchased and incorporated into IBM. iLog created enterprise software products for supply chain, business rule management, visualization, and optimization.

Business units in this company adopted the iLog software to make informed business decisions, specifically to help decide the optimum number of warehouses, locations, products to score, etc. iLog was chosen for its pricing and functionality, which matched the company's requirements at the time.

While iLog can be integrated with the existing enterprise resource planning (ERP) system, the business unit's implementation of the software does not interoperate with the company's ERP. This was based on requirements. Also, due to the autonomy of business units, several different ERP systems are currently operational within the company, making integration difficult. Instead of being imported directly from the company's ERP platform, the data is downloaded manually from various sources and plugged into iLog.

The software was operational "immediately" after installation (as a stand-alone package). There is a learning curve, as domain knowledge is, in some cases, necessary to efficiently use the software. No customization was required, as the software's default package aligned with the company's requirements. There is reasonable support for data visualization and graphics, and it uses iLog along with Tableau for its visualization needs. Once the data is input and analyzed, the generated reports are used directly to make recommendations to upper management. Overall, the company found the software to be highly efficient and observed a payback period of less than 1 year.

Other technologies

The company is also interested in

- warehouse management systems,
- transport management systems, and
- predictive analytics.

Company 4 results

Integration of analytics into primary transportation services

This company has recently started integration of analytics as a value-added service to customers looking for freight transportation that improves visibility into real-time freight position and allows for improved data-driven decision-making in terms of routing. Leveraging the power of analytics applied to historical customer data and current inventory levels, the company can provide a suggestion on which products to move and when. When the product is constant, sourcing suggestions are made as well. This makes for a global supply chain solution versus a simple truckload solution.

Most of the development of the analytics technology used was accomplished in-house. Industrial engineers were preferred to supply chain professionals for the development task. The company is also looking into adding functionality, such as big data, which addresses scalability issues for the future. Data is sourced from customer's ERP system, flat files, and spreadsheets, which takes longer. The motivation behind opting for analytics as a layered solution comes from customer satisfaction and adds to service differentiation and distinction.

Other technologies

The company is also interested in big data.

Company 5 results

Warehouse and transportation modeling

This company invested in a supply chain solutions team that handles warehouse and simulation modeling. For new clients looking for a generic solution, warehouse modeling is performed based on industry and demand-specific requirements. For existing operations, when clients are looking for optimization, simulation modeling is performed to address current capacity and space issues better. In the transportation modeling area the company works with subcontractors in Asia with established trucking operations. There is an effort being made to produce mobile apps that drivers can download to connect centrally, improving visibility.

Cloud

The company is looking for a trade-off between cost and functionality, effectively looking for niche providers that offer cloud-based WMS and transportation management system (TMS) solutions, which deliver 80% of the functionality with 20% of the cost of traditional ERP systems. The motivation behind opting for a cloud-centric solution is real-time visibility. Subcontractors can provide data over the cloud, which can then be accessed centrally for informed planning. One major hurdle the company is currently facing with this shift is poor internet connectivity in Asia.

It is working to move several functionalities to the cloud, including TMS, transport planning functionality, vehicle allocation, day-to-day load allocation, and smartphone applications. The shift to the cloud also offers central management of access control.

Choice of vendor

Before a vendor is chosen for a cloud-based service, all proposals go through an request for proposal (RFP) selection process, which is a detailed 4–5-month review process. Questionnaires regarding the functionality of the service offering are sent to vendors, and a select few that pass the round are invited onsite for a live demo. Evaluation is based on both functionality and the look-and-feel of the user interface.

Other technologies

The company is also interested in smartphone applications.

The next three cases discuss companies that implemented inventory optimization software and the impact on costs, profits, and customer service.

Benco dental

Benco Dental is the largest privately owned dental supply distributor in the United States. It operates in 50 states, with 59 showrooms, 20,000 + customers, 5 distribution centers, and 59,000 products supplied by over 1100 manufacturers.

To stay at the head of the game, it needs more than the 100-pound carry case that launched its success. Since those early days, it has implemented and enhanced the industry's most advanced electronic ordering system to support customer service. To ensure customers always have the products available when needed, Benco has also implemented the industry's most advanced supply chain optimization technology and put in place effective sales, inventory, and operations planning process.

"As a distributor in a competitive market, our success depends on two primary factors: 'on time' delivery of product and value-added services to customers," states Paul Jackson, vice president of marketing, "we have always had very high customer service levels with 94% of lines ordered being completely filled at time of order. The difference today is that we have maintained those world-class service levels, actually taken them to 96%, with fewer people and a lower inventory investment."

Benco implemented inventory optimization in 2007 prior to the beginning of the 2008 recession. With the inventory model's ability to simulate customer demand for every item (SKU) at every location in our business, (SKUL), we quickly saw that our business was going to decline. The inventory optimization model was able to alert us to that fact with sufficient lead time that we could reduce our supply orders and respond to demand without creating excess inventories.

"Its ability to do this was impressive given that 40% of our items are low volume and have sporadic demand," states Andy Thomas, director of supply chain management.

"By driving our Sales, Inventory, and Operations Planning process with the profit optimized analysis, we were able to maintain share growth throughout the recession," states Thomas. "Based on such profit optimized plans and inventory policies, we were able to reduce our inventory investment by 15% while simultaneously increasing our revenues 7% in a declining economy."

In 2011, Benco Dental further enhanced the capabilities of inventory optimization with the constrained service level optimization (CSLO) method. "Adding CSLO," states Thomas, "accelerated our growth in both profitability and market share." Several of the unique optimization and inventory planning capabilities that enabled Benco Dental to achieve their results are as follows:

1. *Dynamic forecast model selection* that tests for plausibility and accuracy to provide an objective demand plan baseline and eliminate as much human bias as possible.
2. *Dynamic analysis of supply and demand for every stocking-keeping unit at a location (SKUL)* across the enterprise that considers all error sources, including the variability in supply and user variance from plan. Only through this comprehensive approach can precise service-level attainment be achieved (most alternative approaches overshoot for most items and undershoot for some, leading to excess costs). The goal is to attain exactly the cost-minimizing or profit-maximizing service level, not more or less.
3. *Profit-optimized inventory policies* (e.g., replenishment order sizing and safety/service stock) calculated at the SKUL level, considering total annual cost, comprehensive error, targeted customer service levels, and all relevant dependencies and constraints.

4. *Leading indicator, extrinsic variable, and viability analysis* to ensure forecasts and plans are not just a "look in the rear-view mirror."
5. *Real-time simulation* to support both the internal scenario analysis as well as to give executives the ability to simulate scenarios for both tactical and strategic initiatives, including stocking policy (what to stock where) and network flow optimization (how best to provision it).
6. *Automated and optimized replenishment planning* that determines the profit and service level optimum source for each replenishment (parent location, primary vendor, surplus location, alternate vendor, substitute, etc.). Purchase constraints and opportunities (e.g., bulk buy discounts or rebates) are dynamically analyzed in the generation of specific orders to meet or fulfill these parameters at least total annual cost, given targeted customer service levels.

Stuller settings

Stuller Settings has come a long way since 1970 when Matthew Stuller first began providing local jewelers with findings (components) on a friendly, timely basis. Today, Stuller Settings is one of the world's largest manufacturers and distributors of fine jewelry-related products, providing more than 300,000 different items to the trade. Stuller provides just-in-time delivery to its account base of more than 50,000 jewelers throughout North America, and the world. Stuller has been able to ensure a 99% line item fill rate by managing its operations with inventory planning and optimization models.

Through its innovative manufacturing and distribution techniques, Stuller has become known as the premier just-in-time supplier to the industry. The company operates in nearly 200,000 square feet of manufacturing and administrative facilities at its headquarters in Lafayette, Louisiana, with additional manufacturing facilities in Chattanooga, Tennessee. To improve its sourcing of diamonds and colored stones, Stuller has established buying offices in Tel Aviv in Israel, Bangkok, and Thailand and entered into cooperative agreement in Bombay, India.

Stuller has also opened jewelry service centers in Houston, Los Angeles, Seattle, Miami, Chicago, Philadelphia, Atlanta, and Toronto to serve retail jewelers in those major metropolitan areas. To support this dynamic distribution network, it implemented inventory optimization software throughout the company. "The implementation of inventory optimization was a quick and easy process." states Stuller's vice president of logistics, "It took about 10 weeks using the implementation templates. By our third month we were tracking profit improvements to our bottom line."

> *Our industry reputation is based on next day delivery of virtually everything needed to supply your local jeweler. Being in stock is not just a financial decision, but a strategic one. 'We carry the inventory so you don't have to' is more than a slogan — it's who we are. Prior to installing inventory optimization software, we tried to keep this promise through a system that generated large surpluses of slow moving items, without preventing high stock outs on the very best sellers. We had 50% of our inventory supporting the last 10% of sales. This morning, we were 99.5% in stock and maintained an average of 98.5% during our peak holiday season. We are also learning that it is not necessary to maintain the huge safety stocks that resulted from our old ERP based system.*

"Our business is a very dynamic business that is driven by holidays and seasonal buying trends. One of the most amazing things is the responsiveness of the optimization planning tools to automatically identify changes in our business," explains the executive director of manufactured products. "Due to some product changes we had made, there was a significant change in demand, causing our service levels to drop to a low of 96% during our peak demand period. However, the software was so responsive that we only remained below 99% for 6 weeks and were then back on track with no unusual expediting. Prior to implementing the software, it would have taken us at least 12 weeks to make a recovery like that."

Several of the unique optimization and inventory planning capabilities that enabled Stuller Settings to achieve their results are as follows:

1. *Dynamic forecast model selection* that automatically tests for pattern plausibility and accuracy to provide an objective demand plan baseline and eliminate as much human bias as possible.
2. *Dynamic analysis of supply and demand for every SKUL* across the enterprise that considers all error sources, including the variability in supply and user variance from plan. The goal is to achieve precisely the cost-minimizing or profit-maximizing service level (not more or less).
3. *Profit-optimized inventory policies* (e.g., replenishment order sizing and safety/service stock) calculated at the SKUL level, considering total annual cost (e.g., changeover vs carrying), comprehensive error, targeted service levels, and production constraints.
4. *Leading indicator, extrinsic variable, and viability analysis* to ensure forecasts and plans are not just "rearward-looking" but incorporate trade partner data (e.g., customer forecasts, point of sale (POS) data) as well as macrodata (e.g., housing starts, interest rates).

5. *Multiechelon inventory optimization (MEIO)* algorithms that determine whether to stock items and at what service level. These solve for interdependencies within the bill of materials and among locations to devise inventory and postponement strategies while meeting customer delivery expectations at minimum total cost.
6. *Dynamic production optimization* that automatically creates capacity and material-feasible master production schedules, which sequence stock keeping unit (SKU) work order requirements optimally given change-over costs, inventory carrying costs, and on-time delivery goals. It also provides strategic determination of target capacity and trade-offs of prebuild versus overtime.

Steel pipe and supply

Headquartered in Manhattan, Kansas, Steel and Pipe Supply (SPS) is a leading carbon steel distributor with value-added processing, coil processing, and logistics capabilities. For over 60 years, this private company has been driving "to exceed our customers' expectations in everything we do." SPS has distribution and service centers in Kansas, Missouri, Oklahoma, and Texas.

Company objectives

- Continue to be known as the "supplier with everything"
- Increase preexpedite fill rates
- Improve inventory turns by reducing inventory investment
- Manage upturns and downturns proactively

Approach

The approaches are as follows:

- Automated forecasting with user exception reviews
- Demand-driven with material network dependencies
- Segmented buy-to-order demand and stock inventory
- Classified items and optimized service levels

Results

The results are as follows:

- Lower days of inventory than five out of six competitors
- Weathered downturn and match inventory to fluctuations

- Spend less time buying, more time ensuring customer service
- Achieve service level targets while lowering inventory

The challenge

The economic downturn of 2008 was a shock for the entire metals industry; demand dropped suddenly, and inventories were difficult to lower to profitable levels. The crisis made it clear to SPS that it needed a new software solution with specific supply chain planning and optimization capabilities relevant to its industry and with more sophisticated capabilities than its ERP to manage inventory. SPS began a search for advanced planning and optimization solutions by evaluating several vendors.

The solution

The vendor chosen identified numerous places for improvement across SPS' entire supply chain, starting with MEIO and replenishment planning. While the vendor identified that the majority of items should have lower inventory levels, there were also many items recommended to have increased inventory levels in order to prevent stockouts or expediting while maintaining profitability.

The benefits

- Optimized inventory: Going into the project, SPS felt that reducing forecast error would provide the largest share of the expected benefit. It became evident, however, that the highest financial impact was due to dynamic inventory policy optimization. Over two-thirds of the inventory savings were attributable to inventory optimization. Service-level improvements also enabled other savings, such as reduction in out-of-territory expediting/transport costs.
- Improved efficiency: Buyers and planners now spend less time on regular ordering tasks by letting the exception-based workflow deal with the typical "headaches" and spend more time dealing with outliers, larger impact areas, and customer service. "It definitely helps prioritize time and energy for the buyers. This system will tell you every day what items you need to replenish tomorrow, the emergency items. That's a huge time saver," said Pamela Jager, manager of financial planning and analysis. In the 8 years using inventory optimization software, SPS has not had to add any new buyers or planners, despite company growth.

- Ease of use: The software continuously adapts to SPS' processes. For example, planners and buyers can manage different parameters by item and supplier when sourcing an order. Once the preferred supplier is determined, the software is then used to identify key planning parameters, such as lead time, minimum order quantity, and order bundles. This gives SPS flexibility and speed of response it did not have before.

> *One of the big differences today is we have a lot fewer surprises about our inventory position. That's important. It's not, 'hey we're out of this.' Inventory optimization software brings light to the emergency items before it impacts the customers. (Matt Crocker, CEO)*

Conclusions

Technology is ever changing. Supply chains must account for this and be adapted accordingly. A chain is only as strong as its weakest link, and not allowing for dynamic transformation in all sectors would only hinder progress. It is hence not just one area, such as transportation or warehousing, into which a company must look to progress, but all areas in the supply chain. With an integrated system of technologies in place, advancements in any one sector—such as better optimization software or more accurate radio frequency identification (RFID) tags—contribute to the health of the entire supply chain.

Some of the key conclusions drawn from these case studies are highlighted below, which represent attributes and criteria exhibited by the companies studied with regard to supply chain technology implementation:

- *Technology awareness:*

  Companies are becoming more and more aware of the possibilities of technology. For example, big data technologies (UPS's ORION) and predictive analytics (Accenture's TALERIS) are leveraged for making better informed decisions. The shift to the cloud is continuing for better demand planning and risk mitigation.
- *Ease of integration:*

  One of the major changes observed by one respondent was that the amount of integration needed with the existing warehouse management system has been reduced, with some products not having to interface with the WMS at all. However, another respondent stated that integration with existing systems can be very difficult. The respondent stated, "The amount of integration needed with the existing warehouse management system has reduced the products that can be used, with some products not being able to interface with the WMS at all."

- *Variety of service offerings:*

  The focus of technology vendors should be on customization, to meet the demands of companies that operate within different frameworks. For example, one company opted for the Fetch Robotics solution as opposed to standard ASRS, based on its requirement and constraints. Another company shifted to the cloud instead of building a traditional data warehouse. Affordability (be it in terms of direct costs or maintenance or associated risk) is also very important.
- *Storage issues:*

  Warehouses do not have the luxury of expanding in the traditional way to accommodate increased demand. Instead, they are looking for space-effective solutions such as ASRS and high-density shelving.
- *The need for real-time reactive systems:*

  One company mentioned is using predictive analytics to predict disruptions and to act accordingly and in a real-time fashion. Increased visibility across different components of a supply chain was also seen as very important for better demand and operational planning. With increasing demand variability and increased cost of failure due to increased scale, automated systems have to be in place in order to react in real time.
- *The need for integration:*

  Integration of technology into the supply chain, once an enhancement, has now become a necessity. Through such integration, companies are looking to
  - improve return on investment by using technologies that better leverage utilization of capital expenditures in people and equipment;
  - create operational efficiencies in order to reduce inventory and improve cycle times; and
  - improve customer responsiveness by reducing lead times, improving product availability, and offering flexibility to changing customer demands.

CHAPTER 10

Technology in supply-chain management and logistics: what does the future hold?

Mellissa Gyimah-Concepcion
Division of Education, Judson University, Elgin, Illinois, United States

Contents

Introduction

The last decade of the 20th century was particularly transient and dynamic for organizations and businesses, particularly in the supply-chain management field. The rate of change is increasing as we progressed into the 21st century, and, with that, organizations have had to be responsive to this change—and at a rapid pace! Essentially, "organizations need to be able to transform themselves to survive in the intensely competitive global environment" (Coyle, Langley, Novack, & Gibson, 2016). Part of this transformation is keeping up with the future of technology within supply-chain management.

Whats and whys of the change: implications

It is important to note how the supply-chain landscape is currently changing; however, not only that it is changing, but what we envision the

Technology in Supply Chain Management and Logistics
DOI: https://doi.org/10.1016/B978-0-12-815956-9.00010-7

future of supply chain to look like. Below are five major external forces adapted from (Coyle et al., 2016) that are driving the rate of change and currently shaping the economy and political scenery:

1. Globalization

   Globalization has led to a more competitively intense economic and geopolitical environment. This is evident in the way that opportunities and threats—both economically and geopolitically—result in the volatility of supply and demand, shorter product life cycles, and the blurring of traditional organizational boundaries.

2. Technology

   Companies have transformed their processes due to technology, and it has changed the dynamics of the marketplace. We are constantly connected to one another, which has enabled individuals and small organizations to create huge opportunities for collaboration within the supply chain.

3. Organizational consolidation

   After WWII, product manufacturers became quite a driving force in supply chains. Retailers and their economic buying power have increased, even among smaller organizations. Consolidation and power shift mean that large retailers are given special consideration from consumer product companies. Also, mutual cost savings and better customer services are arising out of more collaboration among organizers.

4. The empowered consumer

   Consumers today are more educated and empowered because of technology; they can compare prices, are given more choices and flexibility because of the many options to which the internet exposes them. This means that requirements on supply chain have greatly increased as companies are more likely to order more frequently and in smaller batches to satisfy consumers.

5. Government policy and regulation

   Various levels of government (including federal, state, and local government) assert control over administrative policies and taxes, which directly affects individual businesses and supply chains. This has bred more competition along with the need to respond to consumer needs quickly.

This chapter focuses primarily on the future of technology in supply chain, and this involves companies, as well as classrooms and courses. It is a cutting-edge notion that is only just becoming recognized within supply chain, and being explored and utilized in a way that is invigorating and unique, not recreating old systems with new technology endeavors.

Top eight supply-chain technology trends for 2018

Supply chain technology can be used as a powerful advantage, giving your company a competitive edge. It can sense and shape demand. "Supply chain leaders must assess their company's risk culture to determine their readiness to explore and adopt emerging offerings," a researcher at Gartner, Christian Titze, advises. "If in doubt, consider piloting small projects to determine whether the potential benefit of the technology trend is worth the risk and required investment in new skills, capabilities, and services." (Gartner, 2018, paragraph 2).

Technology in supply chain can optimize and assist with the following:

- From your raw material suppliers
- To your inventory
- Through production
- To your end customers.

Gartner (2018) identified the following eight top technology trends in supply chain for 2018, and how they can be used competitively:

1. Artificial intelligence (AI)

   AI has the potential to transform supply-chain processes. AI can be applied to enhance and possibly automate decision making, reinvent business models, all of which could make other emerging technologies obsolete. At this point, AI solutions are able to locate patterns and predict future scenarios, but they lack decision-making abilities.

2. Advanced analytics

   Advanced analytics can significantly impact the demand for supply-chain talent as processes that previously relied on human judgment and discernment can now be handled by predictive and prescriptive analytics. "Prescriptive analytics can improve decision making in functional areas like supply-chain planning, sourcing, and logistics and transportation, and can be deployed to improve end-to-end supply-chain performance" (Gartner, 2018, paragraph 8).

3. Internet of Things (IoT)

   The use of IoT is growing, but only in select supply-chain domains. It is rarely part of a complete day-to-day supply-chain process. This is the exception of air and defense industry, considering airplanes have thousands of sensors and data, which are leveraged in the extended supply chain. Other possibly impactful supply-chain use cases are in precautionary "maintenance, sourcing, manufacturing, logistics, demand management, and services."

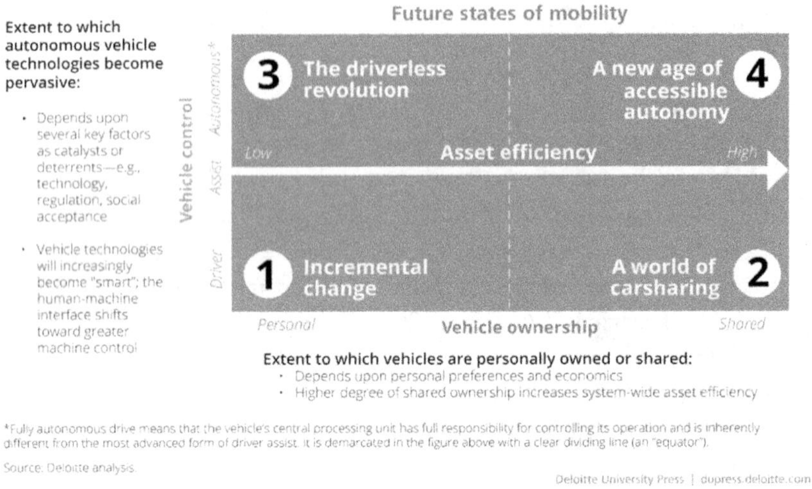

Figure 10.1 Future states of mobility with autonomous vehicles.

4. Intelligent things

    Intelligent things such as autonomous mobile robots and autonomous vehicles (AV) are mostly targeted at specific scenarios and controlled environments, for example, in warehouses. Intelligent things have the capacity to make their business impact across a wide range of "asset-centric, product-centric and service-centric industries." Organizations are thus enabled to "assist, replace, or redeploy their human workers in more value-adding activities that could possibly create transformational business benefits" (Fig. 10.1).

5. Conversational systems

    Conversational systems are most recognizably enacted currently in virtual personal assistants and chatbots. This, in conjunction with conversational commerce, is taking interaction to a new level. They are renowned for being able to handle discovery questions without human involvement, even offering solutions.

6. Robotic process automation (RPA)

    Robotics enable supply-chain leaders to cut costs, eradicate human keying inaccuracies, therefore speeding up processes and link applications.

7. Immersive technologies

    Immersive technologies, such as virtual reality (VR) and augmented reality (AR), allow supply-chain businesses to amplify employee and customer digital experiences. Gartner (2018) estimates that VR will reach mainstream consumption within the next 2–5 years. They also believe that AR may go mainstream in the next 5–10 years, but these technologies are already commonplace in a variety of industries. These include, but not limited to, "enhanced repair and maintenance capabilities in manufacturing, logistics, and warehousing and better purchasing choices for customers leveraging product visualization or store layout and planning."

8. Blockchain

Some highly localized supply-chain management functions, such as smart contracts or traceability and authentication, are chief candidates for blockchain. Many business use cases are still in the process of being proven, but a few early pilot projects have emerged that are experimenting with the potential of blockchain in the supply chain. For example, blockchain is currently being used to track the movement of diamonds from mining, to retail stores by developing a digital record that consists of unique attributes.

This chapter will focus on several technologies that are considered emerging and exponential technologies as discussed in Chapter 2, Technologies in supply-chain management and logistics, of this book. These include IoT since it is a select technology, but a growing one, as well as AV, which falls under the category of intelligent things. This is because many of the companies in the United States use AV in the plant and warehouse, and there has been a discussion as to whether this is or will be replacing human workers. In other words, companies or industries using AV potentially may not be an ideal area of supply chain to go into, or for those already in the field. It will also discuss the use of drones, which falls under the category of intelligent things, and 3D printing, which is within the category of RPA. Blockchain, advanced analytics, more specifically data analytics, will also be addressed. All these technologies assist with meeting the demand, efficiency in production, eliminating human errors, and cutting costs. It is already easy to see the varied impact technology currently has had, and will have, in the future on the supply chain, as well as its impacts on current and future employees.

Supply chain technology: universities and companies

In order to better understand the implications of supply chain and technology applied to real-life situations, the University of Illinois at Chicago (UIC) will be used as a case study. UIC has been working toward including more courses or a certificate program that would prepare its students for the ever technological aspect of the evolving world of supply-chain management. Where technology has the potential and capacity to make obsolete certain tasks historically completed by humans, we need to equip our students in order to be indispensable.

The UIC Center for Supply Chain Management and Logistics (CSCML), spearheaded by Anthony Pagano, has recruited an advisory board of 16 global supply-chain company leaders, providing UIC with their expertise in how they utilize technology in their companies and classrooms. UIC also has 14 faculty members in this group who provide students with their academic expertise and help students garner the skills they need to excel in the working world. UIC researchers noticed that despite the presence of these excellent leaders and teachers on this dynamic team, there was still a gap in understanding how technology is used in companies today.

Through this vein, the research questions became clear in order to pave the way for (1) understanding what the future of technology is for supply-chain management and how it may be utilized in companies and (2) how this will affect employee hires, such as students from UIC.

Focus group methodology

We adopted a mainly qualitative methodology, focused on group discussions and interviews. We also surveyed over two-dozen faculty members and supply-chain global company leaders. It was clear to see that many were familiar with the fact that the use of technology in supply chain is very new and has much potential. However, because of this, they also knew that it is hard to share with people just where technology is headed within this widely misunderstood field.

Research Question(s):

1. What do you think is the future of technology in supply-chain management?
2. How do you think this will impact employment for those in the field and students trying to get into the field?

Group discussions on what types of technology are being used by companies today

The issue of how to encourage students to take classes has been an ongoing discussion. Going back to UIC as a case study, in April 2018, the director of CSCML met with eight people who are on the advisory board of our Center and two members of faculty. UIC researchers had garnered information across multiple companies and conferences, including feedback from surveys and discussions, which opened the door for important discussions. It was clear that many wonderful and highly innovative ways and technologies were being used, but it was also apparent that there were many ways in which it was anticipated that it would be used. Some members even had suggestions on improvements they believed could and should be made.

Discussion 1: What Technologies Are Companies Using Today?

Pagano:	What types of technologies are you using today in your company?
Anthony:	Investment in new data analytics capability. Slow and excess inventory. What do we need to do to access our carbon footprint? No AI just yet... we're speaking to Watson about that. AI is still a new concept for many people, but in the next year or two, we expect to have applications deployed in supply chain and in functions such as pricing in our company.
Gary:	Solution provider is different from manufacturer, so my point of view and experience is different. E-commerce is changing, and the conversation about it is going away. There is a lot going on with automation in the warehouse: machines can navigate with GPS and can more readily be made driverless. They're becoming self-aware and "talking" to each other. The supply-chain issue is widespread. Machine learning is another new technology; it's being used right now to match resumes to job positions; in receivables, it's "we've received a check, let's use the machine to find out who it is." Processing orders now work this way. Those are the things I think will change, and they are already rapidly changing, especially the applications of them. The new applications are now disruptive (e.g., ATMs used to be in banks, now they are everywhere). The blockchain and the many other technologies we are aware of are disruptively changing things now and in the coming years.
Jim:	Drones are doing inventories in our warehouse currently. We have a customer who installs robotics in warehouses for Amazon. I believe there are things we are doing differently today, but in a few years, the list for AI is going to be long. When I first graduated, supply chain was not even in the dictionary.
Vandana:	My experience is different from Jim's. Uber-type apps make it easy to schedule a pickup or perform processing the moment the need arises.

(*Continued*)

Don:	Start-ups and student projects. What are kids gravitating toward? Anything that can be automated will be automated—that's just what I feel. Hopefully we will get smart about it before it happens to us. Feasibility is no longer an issue; viable is the second aspect. We need use cases; it may be cool but we can't make money out of it. We need to embed these processes. They won't be that different, just faster and more nimble. Real-time in nature, faster and easier. The disrupters will be the ones to figure it out. People are changing slower than technology, especially in our business. We are creating technologies way quicker than companies can absorb them, so we are figuring out a culture that can help the employees to adapt. Policies and procedures and doctrine; the challenge isn't the technology, as we have a lot of it. The challenge is how we use it. How do we get other people to use it? As much as people can adapt will be adopted.
Don:	Some of the most innovative companies I saw were driven to change by customers, or by the competition. The customers figured out what they needed and brought it to the company, and the company adapted.
Laura:	Innovation in the warehouse is in the AGVs and the drones; it is not a person counting, it is the drone. It's what you do with the data, but the interaction with the technology and building on systems that we have today. We are taking away some of the thinking that people have to do. RFID is a good example: that tried to happen 10 years ago but it didn't take off. It is interesting to think about why some things worked and why other things did not.

With this discussion, it was clear to see that another question needs to be asked: what would the effects of the growing use of technology have on employers/employees? Many questioned the utility of technology for those who are not able to "keep up with the times" and whether this would cause their position would be made obsolete, or if they would be replaced. Whatever the case, it was clear that everyone thought technology was not a trend and be anything, companies were working to improve it. Another issue that arose was the notion of the rise of the use of technology in supply chain, possibly discouraging mental rigor.

Discussion 2: A Different Kind of Thinking

Pagano:	What do you mean about not thinking? Do you think that's what we are going for?
Anthony:	I would like to think about it as augmented thinking; we are working in conjunction with the technology.

(*Continued*)

Don: A different kind of thinking. It's easier, but it also requires a higher level of thought. We are visual people and technology cannot differentiate as we can; so yes, there is a different type of thinking going on.

Laura: Taking away the mundane day-to-day activities that can be done by a machine but leave the higher level thinking to other people.

Pagano: How do we get people to do higher level thinking? How do we put them back in the labor force? We will replace a lot of people with technology, and those who can't adapt, do you just fire them?

Jim: People are resourceful. When I did lean, it was not about leaning on the people but leaning on the process. People would be a lot happier that way. The problem with the training is to be agile. Say that this is the angle of training. If you're green you're learning; if you're ripe, you're rotten.

Don: We have been taught not to fail and to do things a certain way. However, now we are in this culture where you can fail as you're learning. So, it's almost better if you fail as we believe that you learn more doing this. Every time a business punishes failure, I believe it sets us back three steps.

Pagano: How does it work for the medical supply chain?

JoAnn: Examples of robots used to deliver pharmaceuticals etc., if there is an issue with safety or getting it there safely, it costs money getting the nurses to put medicine into the drawer; so using automated services to cover these duties, nurses can continue with their patients, which saves money and time. Sell-by date on meds is being linked to systems, so meds are used before they expire. Doctors, nurses, etc. all should be able to use these systems that are connected with purchasing and however else these things can help. Automated vehicles to make deliveries to units. However, if you have microunits and outpatient things, then that is a different issue. They do use drones to deliver medical stuff. There are some rural areas that really need it.

3D printing of medical devices; 3D printing organs. There is a huge issue with donating organs. The internet of things is an interesting quandary, since pacemakers and similar products have regulations relating to what patient got what device. Then if you have a pacemaker that is connected to the internet, it would be helpful for doctors to know what's going on and what the patient needs; but, unfortunately, this can be hacked. We may be using cold chain and following it up with blockchain. There are some hospitals that have used telemedicine; that would have helped someone like Barbara with heart failure. They can keep track of folks with a Fitbit and

(*Continued*)

	add meetings on there without having to make the person go into somewhere. Not everyone has access to these, but it would be convenient.
Pagano:	How do they decide on the inventory?
JoAnn:	They probably go on usage. They have the information they and they track it.
Pagano:	How do you plan for a natural disaster?
JoAnn:	They have plans for that. We had a snowstorm and couldn't do surgeries. But they have plans and extra stock ready there.
Anthony:	50%–60% of the medications aren't used or are misused so it would be good to have something that can.

There is a learning process by using different types of technologies across the board within supply chain. There are also kinks to work through before they can be utilized to an optimum degree. However, does this mean that companies will be deterred from using various technologies because they are afraid to fail both themselves and their customers, or is there any promise of the technology climate changing and growing, and companies changing and growing with it?

Discussion 3: The Future of Supply Chain—Its Possible Effects/Outcomes

Pagano:	Here is William, our chair! We have been talking about where we see supply chain in the next 5, 10, 15, 20 years. Can you share?
William:	Ours is optimization with inventory so that when the person goes to the shelf, they get the exact product they need at that instance, with no excess, shortage or emergency. But they don't have additional stock beyond what they need at the time. And that's what our technology is looking at right now. We are looking at big data and using big data. We will no longer need language translators because the machine can learn such language nuances and learn it quickly and store this huge amount of information. Commercial publishers will all do it by machine. It wouldn't surprise me if it happened in other fields, too. We are starting to see replacements for intense human activities by machines. Accounting may disappear. Do you need a CPA? In the next 3–4 years, we are in for a dynamic change. Are we really preparing people for the true business world?
Pagano:	Are there other professions that you think will be eliminated by machines/technology?
Gary:	What jobs won't be [affected]? It's the rote jobs that will be easily erased.

(*Continued*)

William: There are some jobs where all they do is supervise IT people.
Gary: There are interesting milestones in the near future, [including adoption of] driverless vehicles. I remember seeing something about a certain type of job task that will be replaced.
Pagano: JoAnn had mentioned something about hacking. How do we prevent that?
Anthony: One central process unit for vehicles to create different gateways to get in. We try and create a lot of channels and doorways to get in, so it makes it harder to get it. Hackers try and find the easiest way to get in, but having many doorways makes it more difficult.
Don: The security will be built into the network, there may be loopholes, but the network should be able to fix itself or shut down the loophole. People have broken into wallets but haven't broken into the chain because it leverages math and not the network.
William: When someone comes in and tries to hack (we call it Arnold), it not only senses when someone is trying to hack, it also tries to blow up the machine that tries to hack.
Don: It's a big issue for us as a global company to use our customers' data thoughtfully. But now you see more regulation in the internet world.
Jim: I think blockchain will be a big influence. AI is going to be big and the speed in which it rolls out will be lightning fast.
Don: A job that has longevity. Asking the students what keeps them up at night. Paper-pushing jobs are going away. The truck drivers are going away. On the other hand, Amazon may save the postal service.
Jeff: Commerce last mile. Regulation in supply chain.
William: Global distribution.
Don: Which scares me because they will bring the product faster than the customers commit.
Jim: One thing you want in your supply chain is fewer touches. In supply chain, you can't introduce all these things and have everybody win. There will be both winners and losers.

Supply chain and technology—now and the future

From this, and the many other responses and information that researchers at UIC received, they decided to conduct a questionnaire that was sent to faculty members at UIC, as well as the Supply Chain Advisory Board, which is comprised of prestigious companies across the United States. We wanted to gauge specific technology types, and how/if they were used in companies, or taught/used within classrooms. The questionnaire also explored what types of technology they thought would be used in the next 5 years. There were many types of technologies that we could have explored within the top eight categories, but we decided to be more specific with certain categories. Therefore the questionnaire looked at the following types of technology:

1. Data analytics
2. 3D printing
3. Drones
4. AV
5. Blockchain
6. IoT

Fig. 10.2 shows the results from companies that completed the questionnaire, and how much of each of the technologies listed above that they use in their day-to-day operation of supply chain within their companies. We had seven representatives from multiple companies across Illinois who participated in the questionnaire: Molex, DSC Logistics, Novigo, Freight Waves, GAINSystems, and a UIC faculty member were among those who completed the questionnaire.

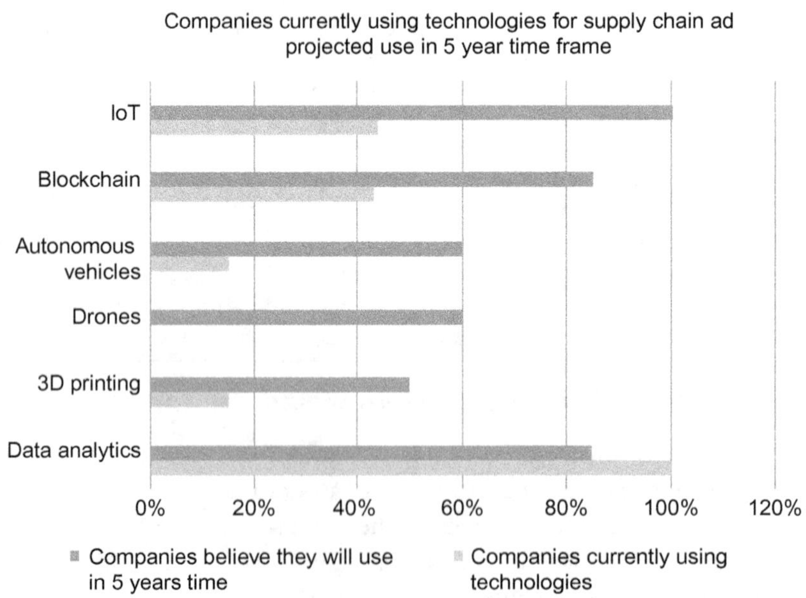

Figure 10.2 The percentage of companies using specific supply-chain technologies and will use in the next 5 years.

Fig. 10.2 shows that 100% of companies use data analytics, with IoT and blockchain coming in a joint second. The least used technology was drones, with 0% of companies reporting its current use. Even still, 60% of the companies predict that in just 5years, drones will be used in their companies, whereas all companies that responded to the questionnaire believed that IoT will be used in their companies in 5 years. The technology that scored high with current use, and predicted future use, was data analytics; that is, despite the belief that it will be used less than it is now, with a 15% predicted decrease. The use of AV and 3D printing double for future predicted use in comparison to their current use. IoT's predicted use in 5 years also more than doubles and is the only technology that all companies believe will be used in their company. Each company uses these technologies differently, based on the clients' need, but they are each a part of a specific industry. Some use optimization, while others use analytics, and others, for example, use blockchain. So, it is important to note that while these responses are a reflection of what is happening within specific companies that have branches in other cities in Illinois, and in other states, the results may not be a true reflection of what is happening in different sectors of the supply-chain industry as a whole.

We also collected company staff member responses to specific questions on the questionnaire to gauge what exactly is happening in their companies. The responses are as follows:

How do you think these technologies will affect the costs of operation of your company 5 years from now?

- "Operating costs from manual tasks will decrease likely offset by costs of technology and technology services. It is also conceivable that overall operating costs stay the same as more technical people will be required to implement manage and decipher new technologies and access to new forms of data and information." *Freight Waves employee*
- "I would expect that there will be considerable increases in capital expenditures while operating expenses are reduced. There will also be a shift from lower wage to higher wage jobs." *DSC Logistics, VP*
- "Efficiencies in throughput, turn time, and increased visibility will lead to slight decreases in overall supply-chain cost. I don't think drastic cost savings, but more consistency and reliability." *DSC Logistics, Sr. Director, Analytics*
- "Significant reduction in the costs from developing products more efficiently and effectively. 3–4% reduction in cost of sales in the next 5 years." *Molex, Sr. Manager, Operation Excellence*

- "At Novigo, we provide consulting services focused on SAP supply chain solutions. Hence, we benefit from understanding various industries and organizations and their supply-chain needs."
  - "We are looking at real-time analytics and actionable data that will help companies make better decisions."
  - "Rapid in-house production with 3D printing, thus saving time and money"
  - "Safe transaction of key documents and financial transactions"
  - "Finally, real-time communications of assets to help drive operational efficiencies"

  Novigo, Sr. Staff Member

How do you think these technologies will affect the number of people working in supply chain in your company in 5 years? Will there be more people, the same number, or fewer? Explain.

- "Supply chain related jobs are expected to increase significantly in my company during the next 5 years as we continue to develop tools and platforms to democratize data within the freight markets. We are also planning to introduce new futures trading products for the trucking industry that is expected to represent a large segment of our operating activities." *Freight Waves, Analytics VP*
- "Should reduce the number of laborers but will be offset by data analysts and mechanics. There will be a significant reduction in the number of workers in the supply chain but total costs will go down less than the percentage of headcount due to higher wages of the new employees." *DSC Logistics, VP*
- "I think the number of people in the direct functions will decrease, but the number of people in the supporting functions will increase, so a drastic change in the type of skill set required." *DSC Logistics, Sr. Director, Analytics*
- "We will have a reduced number of supply-chain professionals with these technologies and with the implementation of RPA." *Molex, Sr. Manager, Operation Excellence*
- "Yes, in some of the adoption of these technologies will impact jobs where automation is the key:
  - Autonomous vehicles affect drivers' jobs.
  - Automated warehouses affect production jobs.
  - Secure transaction of documents and financial information leads to less oversight.

- The flipside: there will be new jobs created by 3D printing. Manufacturing is faster. Companies grow and create more jobs.
- New jobs in the pipeline with increasing adoption in industry.

Note: This outlook is for the next 5 years, which is approximately the duration companies look at for long-term ROI of the software.

Hence, based on what we have seen in industry, there is an effect on the number of jobs but not to a great extent. If this outlook were for a period of 10 years where there is a longer term for adoption in masses, I think that baseline will show a bigger change." *Novigo, Sr. Staff Member*

- "As we are a software company focusing on supply chain planning and optimization software, these questions do not really apply to us." *GAINSystems, VP*

 One member of the UIC faculty completed the questionnaire; the response was as follows:

 How do you think these technologies will affect enrollment in your classes 5 years from now?

- "They will not significantly affect enrollment." *Faculty, UIC*

 How do you think these technologies will affect the number of people learning about supply chain in 5 years? More, same or less, explain.

- "Probably more people will be interested." *Faculty, UIC*

Conclusion

Many issues and angles have been discussed in this chapter; it has been discovered how and what types of technology are being used in the supply-chain field, as well as how to best utilize them. We had contributions from multiple company staff members who currently use technology in their companies, but also how they plan to use various types more frequently based on demand. With the emergence of what is called "disruptive supply-chain technologies" (such as AI), supply-chain leaders will have to decide whether the implications of the technology trends will pay off and/or what those implications will be. It is not clear just how much employees will be affected, especially students coming into the field, but some roles will possibly be made redundant, meaning that there will either have to be a shift in the workforce or employees will have to keep up with the technological demands. It does seem that whatever be the case, the future of technology in supply chain is taking off, and within the next five years, as demand increases, technology may be more heavily utilized to keep up. This means human interaction, and therefore fewer employees, as just mentioned. Gartner analyst Mike Burkett says

> *The supply chain of the future could look like one in which customers and partners may be machines that are acting and negotiating on their own, with little to no human intervention. This supply chain can digest massive amounts of data, anticipate customer needs, predict when critical suppliers will shut down and, then, autonomously and dynamically reconfigure the network to respond, making decisions to qualify and connect, all at the speed of digital. (Gartner Research, 2017, paragraph 13)*

References

Coyle, J.J., Langley, C.J., Novack, R.A., & Gibson, B. (2016). Supply chain management: A logistics perspective. Nelson Education, Canada.

Gartner Research. (2017). <https://www.gartner.com/smarterwithgartner/leading-supply-chains-in-a-disruptive-world/>.

Gartner Research. (2018). <https://www.gartner.com/smarterwithgartner/gartner-top-8-supply-chain-technology-trends-for-2018/>.

Nakamoto, S. (2008, October). Bitcoin: A peer-to-peer electronic cash system. Retrieved from Bitcoin <www.bitcoin.org>.

Index

Note: Page numbers followed by "*f*" and "*t*" refer to figures and tables, respectively.

M

N

O

P

T

U

V

W

Y

Z

CPSIA information can be obtained
at www.ICGtesting.com
Printed in the USA
LVHW011145090919
630399LV00005B/700/P

9 780128 159569